MW00990141

Ellen White on Salvation

A Chronological Study by
Woodrow W. Whidden II

Ellen
White
on
Salvation

REVIEW AND HERALD® PUBLISHING ASSOCIATION
HAGERSTOWN, MD 21740

Copyright © 1995 by
Review and Herald® Publishing Association

The author assumes full responsibility for the accuracy of all facts and quotations as cited in this book.

This book was
Edited by Richard W. Coffen
Designed by Patricia S. Wegh
Cover design by Helcio Deslandes
Typeset: 11.5/13.5 Goudy

PRINTED IN U.S.A.

99 98 97 96 95   5 4 3 2 1

R&H Cataloging Service
Whidden, Woodrow Wilson, 1944-
    Ellen White on salvation.

    1. Salvation.   2. White, Ellen Gould
Harmon, 1827-1915—Theology.   I. Title.
II. Title: A chronological study.

        234

ISBN 0-8280-0818-3

CONTENTS

Abbreviations   6

Chapter 1   The Salvation Dilemma: How Shall We Proceed? 7

SECTION 1—EARLY EXPERIENCES AND MINISTRY IN SALVATION

Chapter 2   Conversion, "Sanctification," and Early Ministry 15

Chapter 3   The Decade Before 1888 23

Chapter 4   James and Ellen: Their Compelling Personal Testimonies . .29

SECTION 2—IMPORTANT DOCTRINES RELATED TO SALVATION

Chapter 5   Salvation, the Great Controversy Theme,
Closing Events, and the Law 35

Chapter 6   Sin, the Human Condition, and Salvation 41

Chapter 7   The Atonement 47

Chapter 8   The Nature of Christ and Salvation 57

SECTION 3—JUSTIFICATION BY FAITH

Chapter 9   Justification by Faith—Before 1888 69

Chapter 10   Ministry After Minneapolis—1888-1902 79

Chapter 11   The Significance and Meaning of Minneapolis and 1888 . .87

Chapter 12   Justification After Minneapolis—From Late 1888 to 1892 .99

Chapter 13   Justification After Minneapolis—Maintaining Gospel Balance .107

SECTION 4—PERFECTION

Chapter 14   Perfection Before 1888 119

Chapter 15   Perfection and Closing Events 131

Chapter 16   Perfection After 1888 143

SECTION 5—AN INTERPRETATION

Chapter 17   What Does It All Mean? 151

Bibliography   157

ABBREVIATIONS

Ellen White Books and Periodicals:

AA	*The Acts of the Apostles*
AH	*The Adventist Home*
ALW	Arthur L. White
BC	*The Seventh-day Adventist Bible Commentary* (7 vols.)
BE	*Bible Echo* (periodical)
CDF	*Counsels on Diet and Foods*
CG	*Child Guidance*
CH	*Counsels on Health*
CM	*Colporteur Ministry*
COL	*Christ's Object Lessons*
CS	*Christian Service*
CT	*Counsels to Parents, Teachers, and Students*
CWE	*Counsels to Writers and Editors*
DA	*The Desire of Ages*
Ed	*Education*
Ev	*Evangelism*
EW	*Early Writings*
FE	*Fundamentals of Christian Education*
FW	*Faith and Works*
GC	*The Great Controversy*
GCB	*General Conference Bulletin* (periodical)
GW	*Gospel Workers*
HS	*Historical Sketches*
IHP	*In Heavenly Places*
LS	*Life Sketches*
MB	*Thoughts From the Mount of Blessing*
MH	*The Ministry of Healing*
MM	*Medical Ministry*
MR	*Manuscript Releases* (21 vols.)
MYP	*Messages to Young People*
OHC	*Our High Calling*
PK	*Prophets and Kings*
PP	*Patriarchs and Prophets*
QOD	*Seventh-day Adventists Answer Questions on Doctrine*
RH	*Review and Herald* (periodical)
SAT	*Sermons and Talks* (2 vols.)
SC	*Steps to Christ*
SD	*Sons and Daughters of God*
SG	*Spiritual Gifts* (4 vols.)
SL	*The Sanctified Life*
SM	*Selected Messages* (3 books)
SP	*The Spirit of Prophecy* (4 vols.)
ST	*The Signs of the Times* (periodical)
T	*Testimonies for the Church* (9 vols.)
TMK	*"That I May Know Him"*
TM	*Testimonies to Ministers and Gospel Workers*
UL	*Upward Look*
WM	*Welfare Ministry*
YI	*Youth's Instructor* (periodical)

CHAPTER ONE

The Salvation Dilemma: How Shall We Proceed?

The subject of salvation continues to generate intense interest among Seventh-day Adventists. It is also a tragic fact that this interest has produced considerable controversy and division. The major focus of these divisive debates has been on the teachings of Ellen G. White.

In some respects this spotlighting of Ellen White's teachings on salvation is welcome. In the wake of the unsettling agitation over the charges of plagiarism in the early 1980s, it is encouraging that once again we seem to be concentrating on the central *message* of the prophet rather than on the *messenger*. Certainly the controversies over her alleged literary dependence opened up new insights about the way inspiration works, but all too often the discussion about literary sources missed the beauty and power of her message.

It is my growing conviction that the biblically based gospel message taught by Ellen White will more than vindicate the messenger. The gospel is still abundantly good news, and Ellen White's understanding of it has wonderful power and balance. Not only does it have power to bring peace, joy, and hope in Jesus, but it can also bring us back to a more scripturally based gospel witness.

The Controversial Issues

The main issues that have continued to provoke controversy are (1) justification by faith and (2) perfection. The meaning of perfection has proved especially resistant to any sort of satisfactory consensus. It has been at the root of almost all the debates in the history of Seventh-day Adventist discussions about salvation.

During the past 35 years a veritable flood of pamphlets, tapes, magazine articles, and books has addressed this subject. All this outpouring of materials has been in addition to numerous official and unofficial church conferences that have been convened to seek clarification on justification and perfection and the closely related subject of the humanity of Christ.

I have actively participated in this study and discussion since the early 1970s. My own interest stems from an appreciation of the sheer importance of the subject and my personal redemption. Such sustained interest, however, involves not only my own salvation, but also a deep desire for the unity and effectiveness of the church. Our gospel witness cannot possibly be effective if we are not clear on what the gospel is but are perpetually wrangling about it among ourselves.

This raises the *key question*: How can we come to a resolution that will bring the desired unity and convincing witness?

Before I make some suggestions for resolution, I would like to ask the reader some questions: Have you ever had the experience of entering into a spirited discussion with someone on Christian perfection and get a "zinger" Spirit of Prophecy statement thrown at you, only to find out later that you had been ambushed with a quotation that was taken out of context? Have you ever had the disconcerting experience of really studying hard to gain a dearly held position on perfection, only to find out that some industrious researcher using the resources at the Ellen G. White Estate has dug up a statement that calls into question your dearly held position?

I have certainly experienced the chagrin involved in both of these bewildering experiences. But my main chagrin has been the distress of seeing sincere people becoming badly divided and at war with one another regarding issues that should be bringing joy and the most heartfelt unity. In fact, one of the really tragic ironies in this whole fractured phenomenon has been that Ellen White clearly tells us that one of the important fruits of Christian perfection is *unity*: "Unity is the sure result of Christian perfection" (SL 85). Isn't that statement an eye-opener?

I not only desire personal understanding, joy, and peace, but also want to see my church united and moving forward in its witness to a troubled and shattered world. Does not the church have much better news to give than reports of disconcerting disunity?

Suggestions for Resolution

I would suggest that resolution should *begin* with intense personal study. And anyone engaging in such intense study will prayerfully take a hard look at *all*, not just *some*, of what Ellen White had to say about salvation and closely related issues. I have long felt that we need to take a more comprehensive look at what she had to say, rather than constantly mulling over our favorite statements. All too often in our repetitious brooding we are only feeding our pet prejudices rather than getting at the issues. Furthermore, this hard look will certainly involve taking care to study her thought in literary, personal, and broadly historical contexts.

The Difficulties of the Task

With these convictions in mind, my first goal was to do thorough research in order to gather all the really important statements on salvation. My second object was to seek the context (and not just the literary context) of not only particular statements but also the larger setting of Ellen White's overall life and ministry.

The task has involved a number of difficulties.

First, there is the controversial history. It is hard to be objective when controversy is involved. The argumentative juices can easily begin to flow, and the usual result is further confusion and division rather than unifying clarity. It would become all of us to acknowledge honestly our personal prejudices and then make an earnest effort to keep our preconceived ideas out of the picture. Even Ellen White herself said that "we have many lessons to learn, and many, many to unlearn" (CWE 37; see also Schwarz 393, 394).

Second, Ellen White left us an astonishingly large volume of literature that totals more than 25 million words in books, magazine articles, letters, and unpublished manuscripts. The task of getting through so much matter seems impossible.

But the good news is that the very practical Ellen G. White Estate has moved forward in the past few years in providing wonderfully efficient research tools. Through the use of the latest technology in information processing, we now have computerized indexes that provide astonishingly ready access to not only the published but also the unpublished letters and manuscripts. Today the serious researcher can rather easily gather all the essential documents in relatively short order. I am glad to report that this gathering work is now the easy part of Ellen White studies!

The truly demanding work comes in seeking out context and meaning. The first task in getting the context involves the sometimes painstaking task of dating certain documents. But again I bear glad tidings. In the vast majority of cases, this can be done with ease and accuracy! When all this preliminary work has been completed, however, the ultimate challenge is to make sense out of the collection.

I would like to testify that while the task is not a snap, it is interesting how patterns of development, emphasis, and meaning begin to reveal themselves as one carefully and prayerfully pores over the collected documents.

My Approach to the Task

Here is how I went about the study. Using the computerized technology, I tried to locate every use Ellen White made of such key words as "justification," "imputation," "impartation," and "perfection" (and their varied forms: "justify," "justified," "just," etc.) from 1845 to 1902. I searched through her published and unpublished works.

In addition to her primary writings, I consulted many compilations, serious research documents, important magazine articles, and popular books by recognized participants in the righteousness by faith discussions. All these documents I carefully combed through for any important Ellen White statements that I might have missed in searching through her writings. I lay no claim to have found every single statement, but I am confident that what I did find gives a clear enough picture so that I can avoid the charge of suppressing contrary evidence.

All these statements I then placed in chronological sequence in an attempt to study her doctrine of salvation in a *developmental* way rather than just topically. While many fine works have been done on this subject, they are almost all topical and doctrinal in nature, rather than primarily historical in focus. This study is *primarily developmental and historical in nature* and only secondarily topical and doctrinal. But the historical nature of this study is not an end in and of itself. It is the means to reach important goals of grasping what she taught about justification and perfection.

Two questions have been raised that I think should be forthrightly faced.

First, when we speak of Ellen White's doctrinal development, do we mean that she moved from error to truth? My answer is a firm "Not so!" When we speak of her development, we mean the way she grew in meeting new and different challenges and how she moved from simple, more childlike expressions of truth to greater clarity and sophistication.

A good illustration of the latter trend in her thinking can be easily demonstrated when *Early Writings* is compared with *The Great Controversy*. The first work is written in the simple style of a young woman who is being led through the battlefield of a cosmic conflict. *The Great Controversy* is a marvelously sophisticated weaving of biography, history, prophetic interpretation, and theology. Yet the movement is not from error to truth.

Second, why did I take this study up only to 1902? The answer is quite simple. Looking through all the literature, I found no pathbreaking statements after 1902. Subsequent study has confirmed my original findings.

Study Goals

My goals have been basically three: (1) to seek to clarify the development and understanding of Ellen White's doctrine of Christ's humanity; (2) to clarify her teachings on salvation, especially her concepts of justification and perfection and the way these two aspects of her thought interrelate; (3) to set forth my own interpretation of her understanding of the humanity of Christ, justification, and perfection.

I do not claim to be the last word on these subjects, but I do earnestly pray that my work will benefit the serious reader and will be a means to bring not only a clearer understanding of the precious gospel, but also the wonderful fruit of unity and witnessing power in the church.

A Note of Explanation

In the chapters that follow I have tried to use Ellen White's own words as much as possible. In pursuit of this goal I have pulled out the key words and phrases so as to avoid a lot of long, cumbersome statements. Thus there will be many quotation marks. So the reader is alerted to read carefully and is reminded that when there are quotation marks they usually refer to the published words of Ellen White.

The Abiding Balance

Before we begin, allow me to share with you my central proposition or thesis about Ellen White's basic views on salvation.

From the beginning she evidenced a clear understanding that justification and perfection are closely related and that the believer cannot have one without the other (1T 22, 23). The emphasis and exact relationship will vary somewhat throughout the years, but the delicate balance in their relationship will be a constant during the rest of her ministry. This balance between justification and perfection can be likened to a seesaw. Sometimes one side is up and the other down, but a good teeter-totter experience will always feature two evenly matched participants complementing and balancing each other. For Ellen White, the balancing act began early in her Christian experience.

Things to do

ORDER PRINTING FROM SALEM BLUE

_____

_____

_____

_____

_____

_____

_____

_____

_____

_____

_____

_____

_____

_____

_____

_____

_____

_____

This Pad Compliments Of

SALEM PRINTING & BLUEPRINT, INC.

475 Ferry Street S.E. • Salem, Oregon 97301 • Phone 363-6097

A Chronological Study

Section 1

EARLY EXPERIENCES AND MINISTRY IN SALVATION

CHAPTER TWO

Conversion, "Sanctification," and Early Ministry

Before we study the critical 1888 era it will prove helpful to pursue some background on Ellen White's personal experience and ministry of salvation during the years before the pivotal events of Minneapolis.

In her long and productive life are three critical passages (besides 1888 and its crucial aftermath) that were especially important in the development of her understanding of salvation: (1) her own conversion experience, (2) the numerous perfectionist, or Holiness, fanatics she had to deal with, and (3) the decade leading up to 1888. In this present chapter we will take a look at her early experiences in conversion, "sanctification," and ministry to fanatical situations.

Conversion and "Sanctification"

The Conversion Struggle—Ellen White was born to parents who were "devoted members of the Methodist Episcopal Church" (1T 9). Their devotion to fervent Methodism, however, did not prevent involvement with another manifestation of deeply felt American religion—Millerism. It was the world of the fervent revival, in this case a potent blend of Methodism and Millerism (and sometimes opposition between the two), that provided the setting for the emerging salvation experience of Ellen Gould Harmon.

Her salvation experience (as she recollects it) began in earnest after the family had moved from Gorham to Portland, Maine, when she was a child. At 9 years of age (1836) she went through a traumatic injury of being struck in the face with a stone thrown at her by a classmate. At this time she diligently sought the Lord to prepare her for death. She strongly desired to become a Christian and prayed earnestly for the forgiveness of her sins. Ellen remembered a peace of mind and a deep desire that all should love Jesus and have their sins forgiven (ibid. 11; 2SG 9).

But these very early yearnings were only the prelude to what could be characterized as her conversion crisis. It began to unfold with intensity during William Miller's first visit to Portland, Maine, in March of 1840 for a "course of lectures on the second coming" (1T 14).* This series of lectures created a serious crisis of soul for the 12-year-old Ellen, a crisis that was not to be clearly resolved until 1842—in the wake of Miller's second series of lectures in Portland.

During Miller's solemn appeals, she found it hard to obtain an assurance of acceptance, feeling that she "could never become worthy to be called a child of God" (ibid. 14, 15). She later related how she felt that she would be lost if Christ should come and find her in her current spiritual condition. It was very difficult to surrender fully to the Lord (2SG 12).

She was so burdened that she confided to her brother Robert that she had "coveted death" in the days when life seemed so burdensome (1T 15). But now her mind was terror-stricken with the thought that she might die in her sinful state and be lost eternally.

It seems that her fears and confusions continued until the summer of 1842, when she attended a Methodist camp meeting at Buxton, Maine, where she was fully determined to seek the Lord and obtain the pardon of her "sins" (ibid. 16). Her resolutions were not in vain. During this deeply spiritual season she came to understand that she had been indulging in "self-dependence." She professed to find comfort in the thought that only by connecting with Jesus through faith can the sinner become a hopeful, believing child of God. She now began to see her way more clearly, and the deep night of spiritual darkness began to turn to a more hopeful dawn (ibid. 16, 17).

While earnestly and persistently seeking the Lord for forgiveness at the "altar" and sensing her helpless condition, she felt her burdens suddenly lifted and enjoyed a lightheartedness that seemed too good to be true. She sensed that Jesus was near and that He had "blessed" her and "pardoned" her sins (*ibid.* 17, 18).

The days following the Buxton camp meeting Ellen witnessed an almost constant state of joy in the Lord. Soon after her return home she was baptized by immersion in Casco Bay and was received into full membership of the Chestnut Street Methodist Episcopal Church in Portland, Maine.

The "Sanctification" or "Second Blessing" Crisis—Shortly after her conversion and baptism, William Miller presented his second course of lectures in Portland, Maine, in the summer of 1842. During this time she had developed a longing "to be sanctified to God" (2SG 14).

Her desire to be sanctified, however, was frustrated by two factors: (1) "sanctification" had been presented in such a way that she found it hard to understand, which left the sensitive Ellen fearing that she could never attain to it, and (2) Miller's second course of lectures created a "sanctification" crisis that caused her to feel that she was seriously lacking in the holiness that was needful to meet Jesus at His second coming (EW 11).

During this time her mind constantly dwelt upon the subject of "holiness of heart." She vividly recollected how she "longed above all things to obtain this great blessing" and have the assurance that she "was entirely accepted of God" (1T 22).

It is very clear that she was here wrestling with the Methodist "second blessing" experience, but more in the context of a crisis brought on by urgent expectations of Christ's soon return rather than the Methodist Holiness revival. Holiness Methodism, however, was never far from the center of her personal spiritual formation.

To get a clear grasp of this issue we must understand that the Holiness Methodists taught that "sanctification" followed the assurance of forgiveness and justification. Their basic teaching was that there was to be a second, definite experience called "sanctification" that was to come instantaneously and was to be confirmed by the Spirit's clear witness that the genuine article had been granted. This experience was variously referred to as "entire sanctification" (or simply "sanctified"), "full salvation," "holiness of heart," "perfect love," "the second blessing" (or "the blessing"), and "Christian perfection."

The popular Methodist expectations concerning the second blessing led the young Ellen to feel that such an experience would "electrify" her soul (ibid. 22, 23). She was longing to be "entirely accepted of God," but she was frustrated by her own lack of feeling.

But her frustrations and confusion were not all in the area of hard to come by emotional outbursts. She also felt doctrinally confused concerning justification and sanctification, failing to understand the meaning of these technical terms.

Then she was hounded by the thought that maybe the blessing was only for faithful Methodists who had not been attending the "Advent meetings" as she had. She was fearful that her Millerite activities had shut her away from the coveted experience that she "desired above all else, the sanctifying Spirit of God" (ibid. 23).

She had not, however, reached bottom yet, even with all this doctrinal uncertainty and confusing emotional expectations. More than excitable expectations and doctrinal clarity were now demanded. Duty, seemingly impossible duty, would thrust her into a final crisis that would bring her search for "the blessing" to a satisfying settlement.

During this time of deep depression it was impressed upon her that she should pray openly at the small social meetings she frequently attended. This was an impression that she fearfully resisted. But the resistance only increased her anxiety. This frightful prospect of public prayer was so forcibly impressed upon her that when she prayed in secret she felt as though she were mocking God because of her failure to obey Him in this seemingly impossible duty. The result was overwhelming "despair" for almost three torturous weeks (ibid. 26).

Near the end of this agonizing period she confided her sore trial of soul to her mother, who urged her to go for counsel to a certain Methodist minister named Levi Stockman. Stockman was a sensitive Wesleyan patriarch who was then preaching "the Advent doctrine in Portland" (ibid. 29). She had great confidence in this godly man.

Elder Stockman assured her that she had not been forsaken by the

Spirit of the Lord. He comforted her with the thought that "hardened" sinners would not be experiencing such deep convictions. He then proceeded to tell her of the "love of God," who "instead of rejoicing in their [sinners'] destruction . . . longed to draw them to Himself in simple faith and trust. He dwelt upon the great love of Christ and the plan of redemption" (*ibid.* 30).

The Stockman interview was most helpful, and she returned home determined to do anything the Lord required of her.

It wasn't long before the frightful duty to pray in the public assembly again menaced her. At a prayer meeting the very evening following her interview with Stockman she was able to lift up her voice in prayer before she was aware of what was going on. The result was that the burden and agony of soul that she had so long endured left her, and "the blessing of the Lord descended" upon her "like the gentle dew." She broke forth into prayer and praises as she confessed that "a great change had taken place" in her mind, and her "heart was full of happiness" (*ibid.* 31). Peace and happiness were the main features of her experience for the next six months.

It is quite clear from this time on that there were no more serious ups and downs in her experience of salvation. Even the traumas of being expelled from the Methodist Church or the severe trials of the Millerite disappointments did not provoke another crisis of soul about her personal salvation.

What is the meaning of her experience of "sanctification"? Was it clearly the classic Methodist "second blessing," which many American Methodists fervently advocated and expected?

The evidence seems quite compelling that in her own mind she had experienced a Holiness Methodist "second blessing" and had found reinforcement of the genuineness of her earlier experience of conversion and justification.

I urge the reader to note carefully the following points.

1. Ellen had clearly experienced a deep conviction of acceptance and an emotional conversion in the course of the Buxton Methodist camp meeting and her subsequent baptism. Thus it was not forgiveness and con-

version that she sought, but a fulfillment of her sanctification expectations.

2. Her confusion about whether she had really retained this acceptance, justification, or conversion was brought on by (a) a misunderstanding over both the doctrine and experience of "sanctification" and (b) the crisis resulting from the realization that very soon she would have to face the Judge of all the earth at His literal second coming.

3. From the beginning of this crisis until its conclusion in the summer of 1842, she used all the classic terms one would expect a Methodist who was going through the "second blessing" crisis to be using. She "longed to be sanctified" (2SG 14), constantly dwelt on "the subject of holiness of heart," and "longed above all things to obtain this great blessing" of being "entirely accepted of God" (1T 22). Her soul was "thirsting for full and free salvation" and an "entire conformity to the will of God." She was in a deep struggle to obtain this "priceless treasure" and its "soul-purifying effects" (EW 11; 2SG 14, 15).

At the church trial in which she and her family were put out of the Methodist Church, she testified that she was not "conscious of any wrong," a classic evidence of the "second blessing" that the Methodists expected (2SG 23; 1T 32). In fact, this very act of testifying about her experience after receiving the "blessing" was also very typical of what Wesley's people expected, and it was an absolute requirement in the American Holiness movement's version of the "second blessing" (1T 32).

While some resist the suggestion that Ellen White had experienced a Holiness Methodist style "second blessing," the evidence seems overwhelming that she did. It is my studied conclusion that the main reason some resist this conclusion is they are simply not aware of what was going on in the Eastern states during the 1840s. Ellen White was caught up in the surging Holiness revival under the leadership of such notables as Phoebe Palmer.

Many contemporary Christians, Seventh-day Adventists included, are not familiar with this remarkable older contemporary of Ellen White. Supported by her fervently religious husband, Dr. Walter Palmer, and numerous leading Methodist ministers and bishops, she had become the most prominent leader of a movement that gave renewed emphasis to a deeply Americanized version of Wesley's doctrine of "perfection."

Entire consecration and a conscious sense of divine acceptance were the key elements of what was referred to as Mrs. Palmer's "altar" theology. This teaching clearly held that the key to "full salvation" or "Christian perfection" was entire surrender to God, what she called laying "all on the altar" that sanctifies the offering laid upon it. In fact, it is this teaching that was the inspiration for the popular gospel song "Is Your All on the Altar of Sacrifice Laid?"

According to Mrs. Palmer, when a person made this full surrender, believing the testimony of God's Word that the altar sanctifies the offering, then one could know that "full salvation" had been obtained— the coveted "second blessing." Such claiming faith and surrender were then to be followed by public testimony that the event had happened. Thus it seems that the "altar theology" was coming into play when Ellen was finally able to testify to her experience of "so great a blessing" (ibid.).

Thus in the setting of the early 1840s, such terminology as "true conversion" and "being accepted of God" were classic Methodist second blessing terms. Therefore, even though her later declarations on sanctification would modify the classic Holiness understanding of the experience of sanctification, they never significantly changed the essentially Holiness Methodist orientation of her treatment of the importance of sanctification.

Early Perfectionist, or Holiness, Fanaticism

Ellen White's later modifications of what were considered normal Methodist expectations for the experience of sanctification were greatly influenced by the numerous Holiness/perfectionist fanatics whom she had to meet during her ministry—especially in the early years. In fact, within the first 10 years of her public ministry, she recorded encountering at least six cases of such fanatical extremism.

All these cases involved self-righteous claims to perfect holiness and sinlessness. And in almost every case the claims were exposed as false, with most of the professors leading lives of shockingly hypocritical immorality. It is quite evident from Ellen White's recorded reactions that all these cases were extreme perversions of the Wesleyan claim to instantaneous perfection.

During this period of Ellen White's ministry, it is significant that *all* her recorded experiences with the advocates of "holiness" were negative. It is now clear to us that the major reasons for her veering away from some aspects of the Methodist Holiness understandings of perfection was the impact of these perversions of "holiness." This was done despite her own sincere experience of the Holiness "blessing."

She especially veered away from the expectation that believers should claim an instantaneous experience and the more emotional emphasis that seemed to be much in vogue at the time.

Summation

What are we to make of Ellen White's early experience and ministry of salvation?

First, the significance of her own conversion "sanctification" crises and experience with Holiness fanaticism cannot be stressed enough for their critically formative contribution to her later doctrinal development. Though there were significant modifications of the details of the Holiness experience, her teachings would always give great accent to the importance of sanctification and perfection. The experience of "holiness of heart and life" were the dominant themes of the bulk of her later writings on salvation.

Second, her confrontations with the hypocritical Holiness fanatics would have a marked impact on the later modifications of her understanding of sanctification and perfection. Her ministry in coming years would move her more and more to emphasize that sanctification was not the work of a moment, but that of a lifetime. Perfection was not to be claimed as some sinless accomplishment, but rather sought as a way of life that would see believers grow in grace until they received the finishing touch of sinlessness at glorification.

---

*Ellen White incorrectly dated this as 1839 in 2SG 12 (see ALW, *Ellen G. White: The Early Years*, 34).

CHAPTER THREE

The Decade Before 1888

Τhis crucial decade witnessed a remarkable unfolding of Ellen White's essential balance between justification and perfection. While she continued to fight a rear-guard action against Holiness fanaticism, during this decade a growing emphasis on justification began to unfold in her writing. We will begin by taking a further look at her dealings with the Holiness advocates.

These later cases of Holiness fanaticism were very similar to those she encountered during her first decade of public ministry. As with the earlier cases, all the later instances of Holiness emphasis on sinless perfection were negative. One of the most instructive examples of these later experiences with the partisans of sinless perfectionism was the case of a certain "Brother B."

The Fanatical "Brother B"

In a letter to S. H. Lane, published in the *Review* of June 6, 1878, James and Ellen White spoke of the condition of "Brother B" as one whom "Satan is pushing . . . to cause disaffection in the Indiana Conference under the pious guise of Christian holiness." They went on to assent to "holiness of life" as "necessary," but censured "the spirit of popular sanctification" as detrimental to "present truth," specifically the "Sabbath, the third angel's message, and the health reform."

In a wry twist they declared that some of the "sanctified" "have even reached the almost hopeless position that they cannot sin" and "have no further use for the *Lord's Prayer*, which teaches us to pray that our sins may be forgiven." They further observed that such Holiness people have "very little use for the Bible, as they profess to be led by the Spirit." The

Whites then called anyone who cannot sin the "veriest Laodicean," and they defined true sanctification as that which comes through "obedience of the truth and of God."

The wry twist was concluded with what amounted to a wonderful touch of ironic humor. The Whites' recommendation for Brother B was that he be "treated at the Sanitarium, at Battle Creek, for the improvement of his health."

It is interesting that they used this case as a summary of 30 years of experience in dealing with the "fanaticism which has grown out of the teachings of ultra holiness." What was it that caused this negative reaction to Holiness teachings?

Although the Holiness manifestations were often quite emotional, the key objection to such Holiness teachings was their proneness to hypocritical fanaticism (ignoring the sober fruits of obedience as the essential characteristic of sanctification) and their downgrading effects on Adventist doctrinal distinctives—the platform of "present truth."

What are we to make of all these experiences? What is the bottom line in all this? The sum of it seems to go like this: Sanctified obedience is very important, but the hallmark of the rest of Ellen White's ministry was to warn against emotional, self-righteous, perfectionistic fanaticism and any teaching or experience that would destroy the doctrinal core of Adventism.

The Anti-Law Extremists

It is indicative of Ellen White's balance in her ministry of salvation that she could not only rebuke the perfectionism of the Holiness fanatics, but also give equally stern warnings to the law-denouncing "cheap grace" preachers. It is this decade before 1888 that signals a remarkable upsurge in emphasis on Christ's justifying merits, but it is always a doctrine that features earnest obedience as the inescapable fruit of divine forgiveness.

The Pacific Voyage of 1878—In the summer of 1878, while on a voyage to Oregon, she felt led to confront boldly a certain Elder Brown, who was claiming publicly that it was impossible for anyone to keep God's law and that no one will get to heaven by keeping the law. He then went on to say that "Mrs. White is all law, law; she believes that we must be saved by the law, and no one can be saved unless they keep the law. Now *I* believe in Christ. He is *my* Saviour."

Ellen White was quick to challenge him in a pointed reply. "That is a false statement. Mrs. White has never occupied that position. . . . We have always taken the position that there was no power in the law to save a single transgressor of that law. . . .

"Christ did not come to excuse sin, nor to justify a sinner while he continued to transgress that law. . . .

"What is the sinner to be converted from? The transgression of God's law to obedience of it. But if he is told that he cannot keep the law of God . . . to what is he then converted—from transgression of the law to a continuance in that transgression? This is absurd" (ST, July 18, 1878).

She concluded by reproving those who "cry Christ, Christ, only believe on Christ, when they do not the works of Christ." And then she directly addressed Elder Brown: "Please never again make the misstatement that we do not rely on Jesus Christ for our salvation, but trust in the law to be saved. We have never written one word to that effect."

Her parting shot was to accuse him of teaching "that the sinner may be saved while knowingly transgressing the law of God."

It is interesting that in reporting this confrontation to her readers in the *Signs* she found it "incredible" that one professing to be a "Bible student . . . should affirm that no man ever kept the law of God, or could keep it."

She reveals to us what was probably the underlying issue that motivated most opponents of Seventh-day Adventism and what called forth such a pointed response: "This is the fearful position taken by many ministers, in order to get rid of the Sabbath of the fourth commandment."

When sorely pressed by what she felt was gross misrepresentation, she declared that salvation *by* obedience to the law is impossible, but salvation *without* obedience is also just as impossible. She declared that we are justified only by faith in the "merits" of Christ, but such faith will never excuse transgression (ST, July 18, 1878).

In relationship to our grasp of her doctrine of salvation, this incident revealed much about Ellen White's developing understanding. Clearly salvation was only by faith in Jesus' merits, but significant obedience by faith was also possible for the true believer.

The European Tour: 1885-1887

Ellen White's years of ministry in Europe were rich in expressions of the great experience of salvation. Her sermons and writings from this period breathe a wonderfully balanced mix, which emphasized the pardon of sin and grace to resist temptation.

But probably the most revealing instance of her balance between pardon and obedience came during the fall of 1885 as she ministered amid the tragic circumstances of Edith Andrews.

This young woman, a worker at the Seventh-day Adventist publishing house in Basel, Switzerland, was dying of tuberculosis. Apparently Edith's impact on the other youthful workers at this institution had not been spiritually positive. But in her last days she had manifested sincere repentance.

Ellen White spoke directly to her regarding her feeble inability to repent "thoroughly," but assured her that "Jesus' precious mercy and merits" make up for "the deficiencies on the part of His repenting, humble ones" (letter 26, 1885, cited in Delafield 89).

Edith died in Jesus on December 24, 1885, and Ellen White recorded this touching comment: "We have evidence that Edith's life is not what it might have been, but her last days were days of penitence, repentance, and confession. We have reason to believe that the pitying Redeemer accepted Edith" (MS 30, 1885, cited in Delafield 90).

Again it must be emphasized that Ellen White's practical theology manifested a wonderful balance. For those burdened with a sense of sin, she spoke of the "pitying Redeemer's" acceptance. For the bitter opponent of the Ten Commandments she upheld the authority of God's law and Christ's power to inspire and produce obedience.

Ellen White as an evangelist and pastor was growing in her emphasis on acceptance through Jesus' merits, but the accent on gracious obedience was never very far from the center of her teachings about salvation.

The 1883 General Conference Session

Although there has been an enormous amount of focus on Minneapolis and 1888, there has been a relative lack of attention given to the General Conference session in Battle Creek in November of 1883. What is remarkable about this session were the sermons given by Ellen White. These talks mainly centered on "pardon and justification" and were clearly anticipations of what was to come to a floodtide after the 1888 Minneapolis General Conference session. They were such powerful expositions of justification by faith that I feel this conference can in some sense be called the "Minneapolis before Minneapolis"!

Up to this time Ellen White had had precious little to say about justification. While her teaching was clear that justification was "pardon" and "forgiveness," it was not until the 1880s that there began to appear this sharpening focus on a more Lutheran by faith alone understanding of justification. In other words, sinners could never save themselves by their good works of charity and obedience, but only through faith in Christ's merits alone.

In fact, the first published linking of Luther and justification came in the *Signs* of May 31, 1883. This development was probably a result of her research for *The Spirit of Prophecy*, volume 4 (1884), which became the immediate forerunner of her classic *The Great Controversy* (1888). This work extensively expressed her understanding of how God led Luther and the Reformation movement in a wonderful unfolding of the vital issues having to do with the "great controversy between Christ and Satan."

What were the factors that called forth this new emphasis on justification by faith alone?

Obviously, the above-mentioned work on *The Spirit of Prophecy*, volume 4, especially the portions dealing with the history of the Reformation, had raised her awareness about the subject. Other factors, however, also certainly played a role.

There were Ellen White's repeated confrontations with the "believe, only believe" advocates. These challenges certainly helped sharpen her understanding of what believing really meant. In other words, justification as a true article must be clearly defined over against the anti-law advocates. Historically there has never been any factor so efficient in call-ing forth doctrinal clarification as heresy—real or perceived!

Finally, the major factor that spurred her rising emphasis on justifi-cation seemed to be her growing sense that there was unwitting legalism creeping into the ranks of Seventh-day Adventism. She detected a pre-occupation with obedience and the law that was practically obscuring the assurance of God's acceptance through faith. This eclipse of assur-ance also benighted the lives of many Adventist preachers.

This latter factor was explicitly apparent in her pointed remarks di-rected to the ministers at the 1883 General Conference session: "I have listened to testimonies like this: 'I have not the light that I desire; I have not the assurance of the favor of God.' Such testimonies express only un-belief and darkness. Are you expecting that your merit will recommend you to the favor of God, and that you must be free from sin before you trust His power to save? If this is the struggle going on in your mind, I fear you will gain no strength, and will finally become discouraged. . . .

"Some seem to feel that they must be on probation, and must prove to the Lord that they are reformed before they can claim His blessing. . . . Jesus loves to have us come to Him just as we are—sinful, helpless, dependent. We claim to be children of the light, not of the night nor of darkness; what right have we to be unbelieving?"*

Summation

During this decade just prior to 1888, Ellen White continued to ex-press her understanding of perfection in a way that clearly differentiated her teaching from the Wesleyan view and its fanatical perversions. But it is also apparent that her balanced views on salvation called for her to turn up the volume in behalf of a powerful emphasis on justification by faith alone. What is interesting, however, is the vital role played by James White in this growing emphasis on the uplifted Christ, who justi-fies by faith.

---

*RH, Apr. 22, 1884. These sermons were published in the *Review and Herald* of April 15, 22, June 17, July 22, 1884.

CHAPTER FOUR

James and Ellen: Their Compelling Personal Testimonies

The strong emphasis on justification at Battle Creek in 1883 was at least partially inspired by James White. The evidence indicates that his experience, just before his death in 1881, had a rather profound effect on his wife.

In early 1881 he had begun to analyze the dangerous direction that the church seemed to be unconsciously pursuing. He informed the *Review* readers of his "unutterable yearning of soul for Christ" and urged the ministers to "preach Christ more."

He then went on to share his intention to refocus his message: "We feel that we have a testimony for our people at this time, relative to the exalted character of Christ, and His willingness and power to save" (RH, Feb. 8, 1881). That he had made good on his intentions was perceived by a prominent fellow minister who noted that "wherever he preached the past few months, he dwelt largely upon faith in Christ and the boundless love of God" (RH, Aug. 30, 1881).

James White's Influence on Ellen White—The impact on Ellen White was apparent. A month after his death she recounted in a letter to her son Willie a dream in which she reported James to say: "We have made a mistake. We have responded to urgent invitations of our brethren to attend important meetings. We had not the heart to refuse. . . . We might have done a great deal for years with our pens, on subjects the people need that we have had light upon and can present before them, which others do not have" (letter 17, 1881, in 10 MR 38, 39).

Speaking to the students attending the General Conference Bible School in early 1890 at Battle Creek, Michigan, she recalled vows taken at her husband's deathbed to stand by her duty. This duty involved bringing "an element in[to] this work that we have not had yet" (MS 9, 1890, In 1 SAT 124).

That the "element" referred to involved justification by faith becomes abundantly clear when the context of this Bible school is carefully noted. It was especially convened in the aftermath of the 1888 Minneapolis General Conference session to promote a clearer understanding of this foundational doctrine and experience.

This powerful emphasis on God's gracious acceptance was not something that the Whites held in a coldly doctrinal manner. The following exhibits poignantly attest to the deeply felt spirituality of Ellen White.

Ellen White's Personal Testimonies

An Infallibly Perfect Prophet?—The last years of James White's life presented some tense moments between him and Ellen. The situation reached a low point in 1876 over the issue of who would define "duty" in their relationship.

After a particularly sharp letter exchange (she was on the West Coast, he in Battle Creek), her initial reaction of indignation softened, and she confessed her fallibility and lack of perfection: "I wish that self should be hid in Jesus. I do not claim infallibility, or even perfection of Christian character. I am not free from mistakes and errors in my life. Had I followed my Saviour more closely, I should not have to mourn so much my un-likeness to His dear image" (letter 27, 1876, cited in ALW, *Ellen G. White: The Progressive Years* 444, 445).

Two years later in a letter to her dear friend Lucinda Hall she again expressed discontent with her spiritual accomplishments. The old aspirations to know "the length, the breadth, the height and depth of perfect love" had come back strongly. She then confessed that she could not rest unless she knew that God was working through her. She also expressed a deep desire to be filled with the Spirit and an earnest "hungering and thirsting after righteousness" (letter 29, 1878, cited in ALW, *Ellen G. White: The Lonely Years* 85).

Once again in January of 1879, when she wrote to her son Willie and his wife, she repeated the more penitential spirit found in the confession of letter 27, 1876, cited above: "We feel like walking humbly and carefully before God. We are not perfect. We may err and do and say things that may not be all right, but we hope no one will be injured in any way by our sayings or doings. We are trying to humbly follow in the footprints of our dear Saviour. We need His Spirit and His grace every hour, or we shall make blunders and shall do harm" (letter 18, 1879, cited in ALW, *Ellen G. White: The Lonely Years* 105).

Although Ellen White expressed the highest goals of accomplishment in the sanctified life and though she spoke of perfection in glowing terms and envisioned significant accomplishments for the faithful believer, there is no evidence of her indulging in any personal sense of spiritual superiority.

These personal glimpses into her relationship with her family give some of the best interpretations and illustrations of what she thought the attitude of the "perfect" would be: always humble, chastened by revelations of fallibility, but eager to press on in the race for the high goal of practical righteousness.

Final Personal Testimony on Perfection—These confessions of fallibility and the refusal to claim perfection were evident not only in times of family stress, but also near the end of her life. In a statement allegedly taken down by one of Ellen White's secretaries and reported by W. C. White in an article that described the last days of her life, she gave the following testimony: "I do not say that I am perfect, but I am trying to be perfect. I do not expect others to be perfect; and if I could not associate with my brothers and sisters who are not perfect, I do not know what I should do.

"I try to treat the matter the best that I can, and am thankful that I have a spirit of uplifting and not a spirit of crushing down. . . . No one is perfect. If one were perfect, he would be prepared for heaven. As long as we are not perfect, we have a work to do to get ready to be perfect. We have a mighty Saviour. . . .

"I rejoice that I have that faith that takes hold of the promises of God, that works by love and sanctifies the soul" (quoted in RH, July 23, 1970).

Summation

In very practical terms for Ellen White's own experience, perfection in the absolute sense was consciously always a receding horizon. In unconscious terms it might yield some definition that was more absolute, but the person in such a state would never be aware of it. The aspirations were always high, but the testimonies were always modest.

What are we to make of the pre-1888 Ellen White? As one moves through her long and productive life, the single constant that keeps cropping up was her great emphasis on God's transforming grace. This powerful accent on sanctification and perfection was certainly formed in the crucible of her Methodist experience of "sanctification" and full salvation, but it was an experience that was greatly deepened by an intense sense of the nearness of Christ's coming manifest in the Advent movement.

The early experiences were central to the formation of her balance between justification and sanctification, both in terms of experience and doctrine. She never seriously doubted her acceptance with God after she achieved "the blessing" in 1842. While there was a move toward a more Lutheran understanding of justification, this move always carried with it the emphasis on perfection typical of her background in both fervent Holiness Methodism and Millerism.

While the details of her understanding of what constitutes an experience of sanctification and perfection would change over the years, no changes in social status, geography, denominational growth, or advances in doctrinal sophistication and expression would change her constant emphasis on God's great transforming power.

Section 2

IMPORTANT DOCTRINES RELATED TO SALVATION

CHAPTER FIVE

Salvation, the Great Controversy Theme, Closing Events, and the Law

The doctrine of salvation does not develop in splendid isolation from other doctrinal factors. If we wish to get a clear grasp of Ellen White's unfolding understanding of salvation, it is important to see it not only in the setting of her life and practical ministry but also in relationship to her other teachings.

In this chapter and the three that follow we will discuss major doctrines that seem to have had a direct impact on Ellen White's teachings about salvation. These important doctrines are (1) the great controversy theme, (2) closing events, (3) law, (4) sin, especially the way it affects human nature, (5) understandings of the atonement, and (6) critical issues related to the nature of Christ (especially His humanity) will be addressed in section 3 of this book.

Law and Grace in the Great Controversy Theme

The central theme of Ellen White's theology was the proper relationship of law and grace against the backdrop of the great controversy. This overarching theme is certainly consistent with her abiding balance between justification and perfection.

The law and grace setting of the great controversy theme was concisely summed up in chapter 79 of *The Desire of Ages*, entitled "It Is Finished."

She outlined three charges that Satan has made against God's character and His government and God's answer to these indictments.

1. God is arbitrary and unfair to require obedience to His law, since this law could not be obeyed (761).

2. Mercy is swallowed up by justice, as humans cannot be forgiven by such a just God.

Both of the preceding charges were refuted in the light of the cross, where Christ demonstrated that God is not an arbitrary tyrant, but a loving and forgiving being who is just in His exercise of mercy. "God's love has been expressed in His justice no less than in His mercy" (762).

With such a refutation, Lucifer then initiated his final charge.

3. God's mercy destroyed justice, with the result that Christ's death abrogated the Father's law.

For Ellen White, this is the final issue in the great controversy. Thus, the God who was declared to be arbitrary and unforgiving is now declared to be unjust (762).

In Ellen White's universally sweeping vision, God has sought to answer these charges with the incarnation of Jesus and His subsequent heavenly intercession, second coming, the millennium, the last judgment, and the final vindication of the faithful. Therefore the gospel is the Christ-centered story of the revelation of the character of God, who is both just and merciful, whose moral demands are absolutely essential to the welfare of His created beings, and whose mercy is unbounded to penitent souls. But His mercy is extended only on the basis of holy justice.

Justice and mercy are but two sides of the same coin of God's character of love. Ellen White declared: "It is the sophistry of Satan that the death of Christ brought in grace to take the place of the law. . . . God's moral government and His grace are inseparable" (FW 30).

Practically all her doctrinal presentations uplift Christ as the covenant-keeping Redeemer in conflict with the devil. This conflict was to wrest His lost heritage from Satan's grasp and to make secure the government of Heaven on the basis of both justice and mercy.

The very heart of her understanding of God is based on the eternal authority of God's law, which is the revelation of God's character of love (GC 493), but this love is not arbitrary and is full of mercy that is just in its expression.

A further evidence to support the great controversy theme as the centerpiece of her gospel proclamation was the very practical nature of her writings. For Ellen White the issue of utmost importance was always the practical application for sin-afflicted humans, who find themselves caught on the battlefield of this great controversy. In other words, the balance between law and grace, faith and works, justice and mercy, God's character versus Satan's deceptions, was the very heart of her understanding of practical godliness and the doctrine of salvation.

Thus the very core of her teachings was the saving initiative of the Trinitarian God, who has sent the Son to seek and save the lost in the face of satanic power and falsehood. In the practical, evangelistic interest of saving the lost, her work was always to exalt God's goodness and to expose Satan's lies.

All this was based on the understanding that this world is in the final stages of the great controversy, and all teachings are to be given priority, depending upon how they inform the faithful about these central issues of law and grace. Satan is seeking to pervert both law and grace by denying one or both as essential to the understanding of God's character of love.

If the mind can be philosophically or practically confused on the key issue of God's character as revealed by Christ's person and work, then Satan wins the controversy. If the mind can be philosophically and practically won to the goodness of God in Christ, then God's loving persuasion carries the day.

Closing Events

Not only did the deep conviction that the coming of Jesus was near provided an incentive to "holy living," but also the lack of holy living was her repeated explanation for the long delay of the Second Coming (Froom 565-581). Thus, to live righteously the redeemed could fulfill a threefold purpose: (1) be prepared to meet the Lord; (2) hasten the coming of the Lord, as the righteous lives of believers would witness to the "world," and hence (3) cease delaying the Second Advent.

The closely related concepts of the close of probation and the seal of God raise important questions regarding the definitions of perfection that God's people must have in order to live through the time of trouble and meet Jesus without tasting death.

For the purposes of this study, Ellen White's most important comments relating to the close of probation and the time of trouble are found in *The Great Controversy*. "Those who are living upon the earth when the intercession of Christ shall cease in the sanctuary above are to stand in the sight of a holy God without a mediator. Their robes must be spotless, their characters must be purified from sin by the blood of sprinkling" (425).

"He [Christ] had kept His Father's commandments, and there was no sin in Him that Satan could use to his advantage. This is the condition in which those must be found who shall stand in the time of trouble" (623).

In these comments are found some of the most challenging concepts in the vast body of her writings that deal with perfection. These comments have sparked much debate and are dealt with extensively in section 4.

Law

For Ellen White the law was God's will. The primary expression, however, was found in the Ten Commandments of Exodus 20. There was thus a rather straightforward concreteness in her teachings on this theme. But such concreteness does not do away with a deep, spiritual understanding of the law. The requirements of the law were seen as "broad and deep, encompassing more than outward deeds" (Webster 92; see RH, Apr. 5, 1898).

As was previously pointed out, Ellen White conceived of the law as being inextricably bound up with the expression of God's character of love—a love that was conceived as both just and merciful. This love has been explained in Christ's teachings and lived out in His life.

The law, as given in the Ten Commandments, has authority for all dispensations of God's dealing with sinners. "But that which God required of Adam in Paradise before the Fall He requires in this age of the world from those who would follow Him—perfect obedience to His law" (RH, Sept. 3, 1901; MB 116).

Summation

What do these important doctrinal themes contribute to a clearer understanding of salvation? The great controversy theme, with its emphasis on the balance between law and grace, powerfully points to Ellen White's call for lives of significant obedience to a law that was concretely expressed in the Ten Commandments and profoundly elaborated and illustrated in Jesus' life and teachings. All this was proclaimed in the urgent setting of Christ's soon return. Salvation and character perfection were not mere matters of passing interest, but concerns of consuming urgency.

More powerful motivators for holy living are hard to come by. These just demands for obedience, however, never cancel out God's marvelous mercy. This mercy was provided for in Christ's death—a death given for the just forgiveness of doomed sinners. The bottom line is that obedience is possible, but it is always associated with a just and loving acceptance.

CHAPTER SIX

Sin, the Human Condition, and Salvation

O ur grasp of Ellen White's understanding of sin is one of the most critical themes to be settled if we are to gain clear conceptions of her views on salvation. If we do not get this area right, it will not only seriously skew how we understand her doctrines of justification and perfection, but also seriously degrade our view of Christ's humanity.

For Ellen White, sin was defined as both *acts* of transgressing God's will (1SM 320) and a *condition* of depravity that involves inherited sinful "propensities," "inclinations," "tendencies," and a "bent" to sin (that is, inbred or indwelling sin) (5BC 1128; Ed 29; IHP 195).

Depravity, Guilt, and "Original Sin"

In the area of depravity and sinful condition, Ellen White's thinking is a bit elusive. Her concept of "original sin" was certainly not in the Augustinian/Calvinistic tradition of "total depravity." This view of total depravity is one of the basic reasons Calvinists teach irresistible predestination. The Calvinistic logic goes like this: Sinners are so deranged and depraved by sin that they cannot even respond to God's redemptive initiative. Therefore, God must irresistibly bestow it upon whomsoever He so chooses in His inscrutable wisdom.

Total depravity notwithstanding, there were elements in her thought that definitely spoke of depravity as the natural, inherited condition of sinful human beings. "We must remember that our hearts are naturally depraved and we are unable of ourselves to pursue a right course" (IHP 163). Adam's sin definitely caused his "posterity" to be "born with inherent propensities of disobedience" (5BC 1128). But such "depravity" is not "total depravity," and sinners still have the ability (popularly called "free will") to respond to God's saving offer.

To briefly sum up: the term *original sin* (with its strong overtones of total depravity) does not quite seem to fit her understanding. On the other hand, being born morally neutral or with natural tendencies to do right also does not fit. In the thought of Ellen White we humans come into the world as tragically damaged goods, not simply unfortunate babes in the woods who suffer lapses of memory and numerous little mistakes. We are seriously depraved and corrupted!

Are We Born Guilty?

With depravity clearly understood, let us now turn our attention to the most elusive element in Ellen White's thinking about sin—the issue of guilt. Human guilt is universally acknowledged, but the question that has most vexed Adventist thinking is Are we born with it?

Some have strongly denied that we are born with guilt (Wallenkampf and Lesher 716). But what is to be made of the following statement? "The inheritance of children is that of sin. . . . As related to the first Adam, men receive from him nothing but guilt and the sentence of death" (CG 475). This statement caused Robert Olson to declare that "we are born in a state of guilt inherited from Adam" (Olson, 28).

The reader may reasonably question what Ellen White meant when she declared that "men receive from [Adam] nothing but guilt."

This issue of guilt has caused much misunderstanding, but see what you think of the following suggestion. Ellen White understood the issue more in a *practical* sense rather than in some abstract, *theoretical* way. For her, sin was stubbornly self-evident in our realistic, everyday experience. She unequivocally declared that "selfishness is inwrought in our very being." "It has come to us as an inheritance" (HS 138, 139).

For Ellen White, sin and its baleful results were ultimately inexplicable. What is all too stubbornly obvious, though, is not Adam's inexplicable rebellion, but our own individual guilt flowing inexorably from our sinful choices: "It is inevitable that children should suffer from the consequences of parental wrongdoing, but they are not punished for the parents' guilt, except as they participate in their sins. It is usually the case, however, that children walk in the steps of their parents" (PP 306). "As a result of Adam's disobedience every human being is a transgressor of the law, sold under sin" (IHP 146).

Ellen White did not feel called upon to address the question of God's fairness in allowing a sinful nature to be passed on to Adam's offspring. Apparently she was just not theologically troubled by the thought that God allows humans to be subject to an inheritance that leads inevitably to sinful acts, which result in guilt.

Again it must be emphasized that her concern was a matter of stubbornly hard practical realism: depraved humans have "sinful natures," "a bent to evil," and "propensities to sin," which lead to sin and guilt. Because of this, sinful humans are responsible for their sins, and this is the main issue that confronts not only the sinner, but also the redeeming God. Thus it is obvious that theoretical questions about "original guilt" did not concern her.

Depravity, Guilt, and Merit

What was very clear in the thought of Ellen White was her view of depravity and its impact on redemption. Human depravity makes the best efforts of penitent, redeemed believers meritoriously unacceptable. This is the very tough, down-to-earth bottom line in her thinking on salvation, especially as she warred against legalism. "Oh, that all may see that everything in obedience, in penitence, in praise and thanksgiving, must be placed upon the glowing fire of the righteousness of Christ"—and here she was clearly referring to "the religious services, the prayers, the praise, the penitent confession of sin" that "ascend from true believers . . . to the heavenly sanctuary, but passing through the corrupt channels of humanity, . . . they are so defiled that unless purified by blood, they can never be of value with God" (1SM 344).

Human "corruption" and depravity always leave the stench of "earthly odor" on even the best that believers can produce. This stench makes their works meritoriously unacceptable. Only what has come from the "untainted" nature of the sinless Jesus has saving merit.

Failure to grasp this significant bottom line can lead to all sorts of theological and practical mischief. A clear understanding of this concept will always protect against any sort of human glory in self-generated merit. It is absolutely clear that we can do nothing, positively nothing, to gain God's favor. Even the Spirit-inspired works of charity and obedience have no saving merit.

Depravity, Merit, and Perfection

Ellen White's very clear teaching on sinful corruption and the taintedness of human effort not only played an important role in her battles with legalism, but also has critical implications for our understanding of how her view of perfection is to be understood.

Ellen White was very clear that sinners will retain their sinful natures until glorification (ST, Mar. 23, 1888), and thus there will never be a time during which the fruits of their sanctification experience will ever be perfect enough to become meritorious. She spoke of *character* perfection (which is carefully defined), but never of *nature* perfection this side of glorification.

But her qualifications were not based on adjusted requirements of law. Her adjustments were based solely on her understanding of human sinfulness that afflicts the entire person—mind, body, and spirit in profound unity. The only solution for this adjustment is the continuous reckoning of the meritorious perfection of Christ's life and death to sinners' accounts. Certainly this understanding of human nature must be taken into consideration in any evaluation of her understanding of perfection.

In the light of such understandings of human nature, law, and sin, how is her understanding of perfection to be stated? She was clear that sinners will never be conscious of their perfection, but what sort of perfection could they have this side of glorification that would be unconsciously present? Such questions as these will be the central theme of the later sections of this book.

This clear understanding of human sinfulness, corruption, or depravity has further implications for the way she conceived her doctrine of free will and God's saving initiative.

Depravity, Divine Calling, Conversion, and Free Will

Ellen White stood very much in the popular American tradition of free will. For her, however (as for Wesley), it is probably better expressed as "free grace" proceeding from God's redemptive initiatives. In simpler terms, what this means is that God seeks us before we would ever think to (or be willing to) seek after Him.

It has been thus since the "original sin" in Eden. When Adam and Eve ran from God in the shame of their fig leaf self-righteousness, God came seeking them!

Ellen White was clear that when sin entered the world, the will of human beings became enslaved (ST, Nov. 19, 1896) and "through the will . . . sin retains its hold . . . upon [humanity]" (MB 61). Thus there is no power in the "unaided human will" (8T 292) to oppose sin. But through Jesus Christ the will of the human being is freed (SC 48).

"It is impossible for us, of ourselves, to escape from the pit of sin in which we are sunken. . . . His grace alone can quicken the lifeless faculties of the soul, and attract it to God, to holiness" (ibid. 18: see also p. 24).

She further underscored this concept of divine calling when she declared that repentance "is beyond the reach of our own power to accomplish; it is obtained only from Christ, who ascended up on high" (ibid. 25). Thus Ellen White was clear that "man is not capable of originating such a repentance as this, and can experience it alone through Christ" (1SM 393).

Her understanding of sinfulness not only comprehended the needs of the penitent sinner at the beginning of Christian experience, but all through the experience of the cooperating believer. "We are unable of ourselves to pursue a right course. It is only by the grace of God, combined with the most earnest effort on our part, that we can gain the victory" (CT 544).

Not only did Ellen White understand the atonement in continuous terms, but she also saw conversion in much the same light. It was the whole process of God's interaction with the soul, not just one initial event, that received the focus. Conversion involved submissive responses (which did not necessarily have to be emotion-laden) to God's gracious initiative and daily submission to His leading, guidance, and empowerment.

Here is the very bedrock of all true experience in sanctification and perfection. Redemption is Christ-centered in all its aspects of calling, conviction, forgiveness, empowerment for obedience (and service) and glorification. But each step comprehends the humble response of the human subject. God was never seen as acting in a forced or deterministic fashion in His dealings with sinners.

Summation

What can we say is the bottom line on sin? For Ellen White, depravity does not debase us to the point that God has to determine everything for us. She was not a Calvinist! She held that God never forces the will. But the effects of sin are so pervasive that we need God's convicting, calling, converting, justifying, and empowering grace at every advancing step in our experience of salvation.

First, our sins and sinfulness are deranging and deluding enough to make it necessary for God to send us a wake-up call; otherwise we would never come to our senses.

Second, our depravity is so pervasive that we need Christ's merits to account us upright every moment of our Christian walk. As our sin pollutes even the best things that we do as Christians, the sober reality is that nothing we could do would ever merit or earn our salvation.

A further implication of such pervasive depravity is that we can never claim perfection in any sense of sinlessness (either in our nature or acts) this side of glorification. Therefore, we need Jesus to declare us "perfect" all the way to the gates of glory.

CHAPTER SEVEN

The Atonement

I t is apparent that some elements of Ellen White's understanding of the atonement are implicit in the great controversy theme, but further clarification is necessary. Her teaching on the atonement was essentially a further working out of the theme of the relationship of justice and mercy as the two essential sides to the coin of God's character of love.

Furthermore, in her teaching the term *atonement* was very comprehensive. It was used to express all that the Trinity has done, is doing, and will do to reconcile sinners (6T 364). For the reader who has sampled widely in her writings, such a broad view of the atonement might seem a bit elementary. But in the setting of the emerging Adventist discussion of the atonement, her views are quite remarkable.

Early Adventist Views on the Atonement

In the early days of Seventh-day Adventism certain influential writers were quite explicit that the atonement did not refer to Christ's death on the cross, but only to His work in the Most Holy Place of the heavenly sanctuary since October 22, 1844 (see Froom 159-175).

The restricted atonement views of these influential pioneers give us another insight into Ellen White's doctrinal and theological independence. Although she did not deny that the work of atonement involved Christ's work in the heavenly sanctuary, she did make it abundantly clear that the term *atonement* also included His death on the cross (7aBC 459, 460).

Atonement and Free Will

If we are to grasp her thinking on the atonement, we must get a sense of the importance that free will, or choice, played in her understanding. Because Ellen White clearly rejected the more deterministic views of the sixteenth-century Reformers, she has often been criticized for applying the atonement beyond the cross.

But given her free-will understanding of human nature, it was only natural that she would see God's reconciling efforts as having to involve earnest appeals and not just arbitrary choices as to whom is to be saved and damned. Ellen White clearly taught that God has provided the atonement of the cross as "a ransom for all," as stated in 1 Timothy 2:6. The atonement is provided for all, but it becomes effective only for believers who respond to God's prior, initiating calls for repentance and surrender (7aBC 468; GW 414).

Thus Christ's intercessory work was clearly viewed as being a part of the atonement. His heavenly intercession makes the implications of the cross effective for believers. As the history of God's dealing with the sin problem unfolds, Christ applies the benefits wrought out on the cross—manifesting both mercy and judgment.

In fact, Ellen White makes the stunning characterization of Christ's "high priestly" ministry as an immortalizing of "Calvary." This ministry thus makes the provisions of the cross eternal in time for the benefit of "whosoever will" (MS 50, 1900, cited in Wallenkampf and Lesher 722).

It would be fair to say that Ellen White regarded the atonement as moving in a line across the history of redemption, rather than involving just one point in history—the cross (Wallenkampf and Lesher 715). Therefore, atonement not only involved making *provision* for the forgiveness of sins, but also *application* of these gracious provisions to repentant sinners.

Atonement involved not only Christ's death on the cross, but also Christ's intercession, which makes His life available to repentant, trusting believers. Such trusting belief not only receives God's acceptance, but is also powerfully motivated to imitate Christ's life. So the atonement has implications for the sanctification experience of believers, not just their experience of forgiveness and acceptance.

Historic Views of the Atonement

I would like to suggest that there is not one historic interpretation of the atonement under which Ellen White's thought can be exclusively categorized. Fritz Guy is correct when he says that her teaching is "a more adequate expression of the biblical witness . . . than is any of the historic views of atonement." Her thinking, however, has some "important similarities to, as well as differences from, the distinctive ingredients in all" the classic expressions of the atonement (Guy 9).

It is almost as if she went on a shopping trip at the doctrinal supermarket and was able to get all the choicest fruits without picking up a single rotten theological apple.

Space does not permit a detailed analysis of all the major views, but we will touch on three that seem to be most central to her understanding of salvation.

The Moral Influence Theory—This theory has in recent years grown in popularity among Seventh-day Adventists. In fact, this view has become so compelling for many that they have tried to make it the dominant, controlling view in Ellen White's presentations on the atonement.

The moral influence advocates lay great emphasis on Christ's death as a manifestation of God's love to a lost world. In its most extreme form it has been proclaimed that Christ's death as a *requirement* of God's justice (Christ's death satisfying divine justice) was not necessary. These advocates hold that Christ's death was given only to demonstrate God's love, which emanates in "moral influence" to an alienated world.

What are we to make of this theory?

It is certainly true that Ellen White saw the cross as the supreme manifestation of God's love. There are elements of loving moral influence that are communicated both to sinners and the unfallen beings of the universe: "Through the cross, man was drawn to God," and the sinner "was drawn from the stronghold of sin." The "cross speaks . . . to worlds unfallen . . . of His great love wherewith He has loved us" and "is the unanswerable argument as to the changeless character of the law of Jehovah" (7aBC 470, 471).

But the cross speaks of more than mercy. Among other things, it also speaks of a powerful condemnation of sin by the "holy love of a holy God" (Guy 10). Ellen White's comments make it clear that "moral influence" was always connected with this convicting holiness of God, not just some general expression of forgiving love that excludes the "satisfaction" of divine justice.

At the risk of being repetitious, let us get the point of God's holiness clear in our minds: The merciful "moral influence" of Christ's atoning death is beyond question, but such manifestations of "influential" love came through God's holy justice, not to its exclusion! Expressions of God's love are always based on *both* divine justice and mercy (not on mercy alone).

At this point it is important for us to ask What is "wrath"? It seems that what makes the more extreme forms of the moral influence theory attractive are the unsavory connotations that go along with God's justice being expressed as wrath. The word "wrath" seems to conjure up visions of God losing His temper, giving sinners "the back of His hand," suggesting that He gets some retaliatory, tit-for-tat satisfaction out of destroying sinners.

But Ellen White's view of God's wrath is that He must finally act to put an end to those who reject His offers of a just mercy. In the writings of Ellen White there are just too many indications of God's active wrath to say that He is too merciful to destroy sinners actively.

Now, there are certainly statements to the effect that sin is self-destructive (GC 35, 36). And sin is manifestly self-destructive. But let us pursue Ellen White's treatment of the theme of God's justice a bit further.

Is it not a fact that God is the source of all life? Is it not His restraining power over the forces of evil that gives us protection? Furthermore, is not God the one who temporarily grants self-destructing sinners life in probationary time? I do believe the answers are obvious.

Now let us go a step further. Doesn't it seem that God would be just as surely responsible for the death of sinners by withdrawing His life-giving power as He would be in directly destroying them by the fires of hell?

Since God is the source of all life, it is quite apparent that He is also ultimately the one who allows death! And whether such death is actively brought on or passively allowed really makes no difference if one wants to lift the ultimate responsibility for the death of sinners from God. The really definitive question is not whether God's justice is active or passive, but whether it is just and consistent with His character of merciful love.

Another nettlesome question rears its wondering head: Was the destruction of Sodom and Gomorrah simply the chance circumstance of an unfortunate conspiracy of atmospheric conditions (Gen. 19:24)? Ellen White says, "The Lord rained brimstone and fire out of heaven" (PP 162). Again, was the judgment of God on Korah, Dathan, and Abiram only a tragic yawning of a long dormant seismic geological fault line in the Sinai desert (Num. 16:23-35)? Ellen White calls this judgment "the signal manifestation of God's power" (ibid. 401). Or were the deaths of Ananias and Sapphira only timely coronaries (Acts 5:1ff.)? Ellen White refers to their deaths as "the signal manifestation of the wrath of God" (AA 73) and goes on to say that "the same God who punished them, today condemns all falsehood" (ibid. 76). Will the lake of fire be merely a passive act on God's part? Referring to the lake of fire, Ellen White says that "God is to the wicked a consuming fire" (GC 673).

Was divine wrath manifested at the cross? Yes, what about the cross? Was it or was it not a manifestation of God's holy wrath against sin?

If the plain, straightforward words of Ellen White mean anything, the following challenge needs to be squarely faced: Any well-meaning person who feels that the moral influence theory cancels out the substitutionary theory of atonement as a manifestation of God's wrath against sin needs to be prepared to rip the chapter "Calvary" out of The Desire of Ages. I realize that my challenge is a bit shocking, but sometimes words are just too plain to be ignored!

Please carefully note the following citations from this climactic chapter of Ellen White's most spiritual work:

"Upon Christ as our substitute and surety was laid the iniquity of us all. . . . The guilt of every descendant of Adam was pressing upon His heart. The wrath of God against sin, the terrible manifestation of His displeasure because of iniquity, filled the soul of His Son with consternation. . . . Salvation for the chief of sinners was His theme. But now with the terrible weight of guilt He bears, He cannot see the Father's reconciling face. . . .

"Christ felt the anguish which the sinner will feel when mercy shall no longer plead for the guilty race. It was the sense of sin, bringing the *Father's wrath* upon Him as man's substitute, that made the cup He drank so bitter, and broke the heart of the Son of God" (753; italics supplied).

"He, the Sin Bearer, *endures the wrath of divine justice*, and for thy sake becomes sin itself" (756; italics supplied).

And is God's wrath active or passive? In addition to these forcefully clear statements, Ellen White makes it abundantly evident that there is precious little emphasis on God's passive justice.

"Justice demands that sin be not merely pardoned, but the death penalty *must* be executed. God, in the gift of His only begotten Son, met both these requirements. By dying in man's stead, Christ *exhausted the penalty and provided a pardon*" (7aBC 470; italics supplied).

"As Christ bore the sins of every transgressor so the sinner who will not believe in Christ as his personal Saviour . . . will bear the penalty of his transgression" (*ibid.* 471).

Is there any substantive difference between pulling a plug on somebody's life-support system and switching on the "juice" to an electric chair? Again, I believe the answer is self-evident! For Ellen White, our God is love, but His love is expressed actively in justice, not just passively.

He is certainly our "friendly" and neighborly "God,"* but He is more than just some benignantly concerned neighbor poignantly beckoning over the back fence and pleading with us to knock off the foolishness of our romp in the fields of sin. He is also the Holy God who has acted and will once again act in just wrath against the rejecters of His merciful offer of redemption. Again there are too many references to God's active execution of justice to say that justice is merely a passive "letting us go."

And then there is that matter of salvation and God's wrath. What does all this have to say about salvation? I would suggest that the redemptive message of God is this: Our rejection of His offer of life through the justifying merits of Christ's death will mean our eternal death. Without Christ's substitutionary death, sinners will receive just retribution.

Let me sum it up: It is God's just love, not some cheap, mushy mercy, that saves from eternal death. Such a conclusion leads us to consideration of the next classic theory.

The Satisfaction Theory—The burden of this theory is to emphasize that God's justice requires satisfaction and that Christ's death brought just recompense for sin. The issue here is not God's sovereign prestige, but His character of love (Guy 9). God is not trying to prove that He is a hard-to-satisfy boss, but is maintaining the justice of His love.

While Ellen White clearly spoke of the demands of the law (God's just expression of love) being "satisfied" (7aBC 461, 465), the point is not some totaling up of a quantity of sin that requires an equal suffering (Guy 9, 10). In the final analysis the issue is God being seen as a just law-giver and the law as an expression of His character that is satisfied (see 7aBC 470, 473).

The Penal-Substitutionary Theory—This theory is very closely related to the satisfaction view. Both emphasize the justice of God in His love. The substitutionary theory has probably been the most popular atonement model among conservative Christians since the days of the Protestant Reformation. The gist of it goes like this: God's justice demands a penalty for the transgression of His will, and Christ's death was the penalty that is substituted for the sinner's just reward.

This theory is the dominant theme in Ellen White's thoughts about the atonement. Christ is the sinner's substitute in that He bore the penalty to satisfy the holy requirements of God's justice. And it was usually in this penal-substitutionary context that she discussed the theme of justification by faith. The essence of the thought is that God can justify sinners because Jesus has satisfied God's just requirement in both obedience to and bearing the penalty of the broken law by being the substitute (7aBC 465).

Regarding the penal-substitutionary theory, Fritz Guy has perceptively pointed out that "the death of Jesus is not God making someone *else* 'pay the penalty' instead of *us*; it is God taking the penalty on *him*-

self" (Guy 11). Jesus willingly paid this price not only to secure our redemption but also to demonstrate the fullness of divine love to a confused universe.

Summation

These different theories, or models, were stated by Ellen White in mutually complementary, not contradictory, ways. But again it must be emphasized that the focus of her atonement thought was centered in the concepts of penalty, substitution, and satisfaction. These became the basis of justification by faith, a justification that condemns sin, forgives the sinner, and vindicates God's law as a just expression of His character and dealings with sin.

The atonement, however, has implications for Christian experience that flow from the work Christ has done for us. These implications also involve the work that Christ does in us. The concepts of penalty, substitution, and satisfaction become the foundation for all significant victory over our sinful natures and habits of sin. God's just forgiveness is the moral influence that inspires the development of Christlike characters.

In other words, at the heart of her atonement thought was the balance between law and grace, justice and mercy, and the demonstration of this right relationship in Christ's life—and ultimately in the believer. Thus Christ's death became the basis of a cosmic vindication of God. This balancing of justice and mercy is revealed in all that God does to bring about the reconciliation of sinners in a truly profound atonement.

What Is the Point?—What is the bottom line of Ellen White's atonement thought? Without a powerful sense of retributive justice, justification by faith dissolves into sentimental indulgence. It is only the penal-substitutionary model that satisfactorily reveals the justness of God's love—a vigorously powerful love that in no way inhibits boundless manifestations of mercy. Far from it!

One simply cannot read the chapter "Gethsemane" in *The Desire of Ages* without being struck with two compelling factors: (1) the penal-substitutionary view of the atonement is always the assumption that undeifies her exposition and (2) many sentences and phrases speak of the intensely costly suffering of the Son of man. Take a thoughtful and reflective half hour and see for yourself.

Jesus' mental agony of Gethsemane and His experience on the cross reveal the acutely agonized suffering of the Son of God in bearing the Father's retributive wrath. Such unparalleled suffering speaks to sinners of a redemption that involves inconceivable costs. If forgiveness is a matter of mere unwarranted gratuity or mushy, sentimental indulgence on God's part, justification is cheapened and redemption becomes only an interesting novelty.

But the writings of Ellen White on the atonement far transcend mere tragic novelty. Her descriptions and reflections do not merely evidence some gratuitous or sentimental love. To the contrary, her poignant portrayals disclose an infinitely costly grace that is more precious than anything in the universe: Our eternal life demanded the very life of the Son of God! No cheap grace here!

---

*See A. Graham Maxwell's *Servants or Friends*. I took this metaphor of God the friendly neighbor from an advertisement for this book that appeared in a recent edition of *Christianity Today*.

CHAPTER EIGHT

The Nature of Christ and Salvation

T he development of Ellen White's understanding of the nature of Christ (theologically referred to as Christology) was closely bound up with her understanding of salvation. In fact, for us to understand her doctrine of salvation, it is absolutely necessary to take into consideration her Christology. This is especially pivotal when it comes to her understanding of the relationship between Christ's human nature and Christian perfection.

The study of Christ's nature is easily the most difficult and challenging theme we will deal with in this book. To anyone who has ever made a concerted attempt at an in-depth study of the nature of Christ, the truthfulness of the following statement is all too obvious: "Man cannot define this wonderful *mystery*—the blending of the two natures. . . . It can never be explained" (7BC 904, italics supplied).

But we also have the promise that the student who persists will be richly rewarded: "The study of the incarnation of Christ is a fruitful field, which will repay the searcher who digs deep for hidden truth" (YI, Oct. 13, 1898).

Another reason for the difficulty of this subject is its very controversial history. The controversies in Seventh-day Adventism regarding Ellen White's understanding of Christ's humanity go back to the 1890s, but they took on renewed vigor with the publication of the book *Seventh-day Adventists Answer Questions on Doctrine* in 1957. The debate has continued unabated since then, and a satisfactory consensus has been very hard to achieve.

In addition to its mystery and its controverted history, three other factors make this subject especially challenging. First, there is the sheer bulk of Ellen White's writings, and second, the lack of a systematic treatment of this subject in any particular article or book. Third, these difficulties are further complicated by numerous complex statements that give her Christology an intricate balance between "pre-Fall" sinless "uniqueness" and "post-Fall" "identity" with our "sinful nature."

Depth, controversy, and complexity notwithstanding, we should not be deterred in this important quest for understanding. The issue is too central simply to be ignored.

So the reader is encouraged to come patiently but also prayerfully and respectfully, remembering "to heed the words spoken by Christ to Moses at the burning bush, 'Put off thy shoes from off thy feet, for the place whereon thou standest is holy ground.'" Truth is then best served if we take off our argumentative, opinionated "shoes" and come "with the humility of a learner, with a contrite heart" (QOD 647).

The Basic Issue

Ellen White's basic proposition is aptly summed up in the following statement: "Christ reaches us where we are. He took our nature and overcame, that we through taking His nature might overcome. Made 'in the likeness of sinful flesh,' He lived a sinless life" (DA 311, 312). The key question is: *In the thought of Ellen White, just how much like sinful human nature is Christ's human nature?*

The more traditional post-Fall interpreters have tended to read Ellen White as emphasizing the *similarities*, seeing Christ as sinful in nature (though not in action), whereas the seeming majority of more recent interpreters are pre-Fall and have stressed the *differences*—the uniqueness of the sinlessness of His nature and life.

Eric C. Webster is certainly correct when he reminds us that "almost every area of belief is influenced by one's departure point regarding the nature of Christ" (50). This is especially true of such important salvation issues as justification, sanctification, the atonement, the purpose of the great controversy theme, and the nature of sin.

Study Objectives

Our first objective is to shed light on the lingering debate over the nature of Christ by seeking to demonstrate how Ellen White's understanding unfolded in her ministry before and after 1888. But our ultimate objective will be to clarify how her understanding of Christ's nature influenced her teachings on salvation, especially during the critical years following 1888.

While the deity of Christ and Adventism's experience with anti-Trinitarian views are dealt with briefly, the bulk of the space in this chapter deals with the development of her understanding of Christ's human nature.

Deity and the Trinity

Ellen White decisively believed in the full deity of Christ. She can be characterized as Trinitarian in her convictions, even from her earliest years (QOD 641-646; Ev 613-617).

What is truly remarkable about her Trinitarian views is that she held them at a time when many of the leading nineteenth-century Adventist ministers had strong Arian influences. Arianism[1] is an ancient heresy which denies that Jesus has existed coeternally with God the Father. It teaches that Christ was created, and thus there was a time He did not exist.

Furthermore, it is of some interest to note that among these anti-trinitarian ministers was none other than her own husband. James White came from the Christian Connexion Church, which had strong Arian tendencies, and some of his early statements revealed an anti-Trinitarian bias (Webster 34).

But despite these strong influences, Ellen White went on her own independent way, quite willing to go against the grain of the Arianism that was abundantly apparent among Adventist ministers of her time (ibid. 72).

She never reprimanded or directly corrected any of these persons for their Arian views, but she became increasingly explicit in her own forthright declarations of Christ's full deity and her clear affirmations of the trinity.

For the purposes of this study, it needs to be clearly stated that by the time of the 1888 Minneapolis General Conference session, Ellen White was forcefully affirming the full, eternal deity of Christ.

Christology After 1888

What follows is an overview of important statements in Ellen White's unfolding understanding of Christ's nature and the ways she employed them in her expositions on salvation during the most important period of her expositions on issues related to salvation.

What is rather shocking about the formation of her understanding is that there were really no striking or pathbreaking developments in her teaching on Christology during this period. I refer to this lack of development as "remarkable" in the sense that there has been so much debate about the impact of her Christology on her teachings about salvation. The simple facts are that developments in her understanding of Christ's humanity played no appreciably significant role in her great emphasis on justification and sanctification that came in the years following 1888.

The reader might therefore wonder why we even need this chapter. I would suggest two reasons for the following study: (1) further attention will help clarify her usage of Christ's humanity in her powerful initiative to emphasize the centrality and primacy of a balanced presentation on salvation, and (2) attention to her most important statements will confirm that the post-1888 statements on the nature of Christ were only further elaborations of what was already clearly in place before 1888. I do this consciously, over against the claims of individuals who have tried to convince us that Christology was the significant thing about the great emphasis on salvation coming out of the Minneapolis General Conference session.

Christology is most certainly always at the base of Ellen White's teachings about salvation, but serious theological emphasis on Christology was not the major salvation feature that fed into or arose out of the Minneapolis crisis.[2]

Developments From 1889 to 1895—About the only notable impact that Ellen White's unfolding understanding of the nature of Christ made on her great presentations about salvation following 1888 is found in the following theme: Christ's nature was vigorously presented as a mysterious blending, or union, of humanity and deity; such a blending was deemed essential to Christ's uniquely saving work. In other words, this significant development arises as much, if not more, out of a sharpening emphasis on the significance of His deity, not just His humanity!

In a sermon given on June 19, 1889 (7BC 904), she proclaimed that "Christ could have done nothing during His earthly ministry in saving fallen man if the divine had not been blended with the human." She further declared that "man cannot define this wonderful mystery—the blending of the two natures. . . . It can never be explained." This declaration that a union of humanity and Deity was essential to the atonement became a frequently repeated theme for the balance of her ministry.

It should come as no surprise to us that this theme emphasized the importance of His deity and His sinless humanity as essential to His role as justifying Saviour. Only Jesus "could have paid the penalty of sin" and borne "the sins of every sinner; for all transgressions were imputed unto him" (RH, Dec. 20, 1892). Thus the *uniqueness* of Jesus was emphasized not just in terms of His sinlessness, but also in terms of the blending of the human and divine.

Christ's Humanity: What Does It Mean?

We find elements of mystery and *seemingly* irregular features in Ellen White's view of Christ's humanity. Some have even concluded that she was simply contradictory in her thought. I feel that this conclusion is not only harsh, but also represents a lack of appreciation for two key elements in her thought.

Central Factors in Ellen White's Christology—The first element is the striking doctrinal consistency in her large body of writings that was produced throughout the course of six decades by a thinker who was not attempting to do an academic, systematic, or technically doctrinal work.

Her comments on the nature of Christ are not contained in any one major work but are scattered throughout her writings, often showing up in rather surprising settings. My observation is similar to Eric C.

Webster's: "The general consistency in Ellen White's views over a considerable span of time is a testimony to her clarity of thought" (149).

The second factor is that not only are her views noncontradictory, but I would strongly suggest that these seemingly irregular features are what give her thought its power and depth. Ellen White could sound like the author of the book of Hebrews when she discussed Christ's profound *identity* with humanity and like John the Beloved (John 8:46) when she discussed His amazing *uniqueness*.

Causes for Misunderstanding—The problems in understanding Ellen White have arisen when interpreters have wanted to stress one aspect of His humanity to the neglect of the other or when they have wanted to totally solve a mystery that cannot be solved by human minds. If there were no mystery, what need would there be for faith?

For Ellen White, the stress on Christ's uniqueness or identity seemed to depend largely on what doctrinal issue she was dealing with. When she spoke of victory over sin and Christ's power to sustain struggling sinners, she was more likely to emphasize *identity*. When she spoke of Christ as a sinless, sacrificial substitute and one who is able to free from the guilt of sin, she would emphasize *uniqueness*.

Christ's Sinless Uniqueness and "Sinful Nature"—Though His "spiritual nature was free from every taint of sin" (QOD 653), He was a rather typical first-century human being. It seems best to express the freedom of His "spiritual nature" from sin this way: He was *affected* by sin but not *infected* with it.

Ellen White was clear that He took a "sinful nature" (*ibid.* 657), but only in the sense of a *lessened capacity* because of the principle of physical inheritance. He was weak, frail, infirm, degraded, degenerate, deteriorated, wretched, and defiled, but somehow He was *not* "altogether human, such an one as ourselves; for it cannot be" (5BC 1129).

Whatever this *lessened capacity* involved, it did *not* involve yielding to corruption (He never sinned by an act of sin) or inclinations to corruption, a "taint of sin," or "an evil propensity" in His sinless "spiritual nature" (QOD 651, 653). Although Christ was not just like fallen humans, He was enough like them to identify with their "infirmities" in the struggle with temptation. His nature, however, was enough unlike them to be a sinless, substitutionary sacrifice.

The arguments of those who claim that Christ had to be *just exactly like* sinful humans in order to identify with them breaks down over one stubborn fact of human history: *we have all sinned, but Christ never did.* Think about that for a moment.

The power of temptation is always strengthened by a previous experience in sin. The temptation to commit that sin will be more powerful for those who have succumbed than for someone who has never indulged in it. Does this make Christ unable to help us or identify with us in our temptations?

Eric Webster forcefully lays out the inexorable logic of the situation: "Right here there remains a massive gap between Christ and the sinner. At best, Christ can only face initial temptation, but He cannot be brought down to the level of the alcoholic who faces the temptation to indulge in strong drink for the thousandth time. . . . Christ never knew the power of habitual sin and cannot meet fallen man on that level," and any attempt to drag Him down fully to our level collapses "on the bedrock of" our history of universally "habitual sin" (419, 420).

Can Christ really identity with us?—Let's face the practical issue squarely: If Christ's *identity* involves no history of habitual sin and not being born with "tendencies" and "propensities" to sin, how, then, can He really identify with us in our struggle with temptation? Can He really help us who are born with such tragic histories and corrupt, depraved "tendencies"?

I would suggest that Christ did not need to be born with either a bent to sin or have a history of sinning to feel the power of temptation. Upon further reflection it becomes obvious that the basis of His temptations was not a corrupt nature or sordid history of sin, but the possibility of using His own inherent full deity to resist the wiles of the devil.

In other words, the key temptation for Christ was the same as it is for all humans—the desire to go it alone and depend upon self rather than divinely imparted power from above. The history of Adam and Eve, along with one third of the heavenly angels, ought to give us a clue about a simple fact of human experience: *having natural tendencies to sin is not essential to being tempted.* Certainly God did not create them flawed in this way!

Morris Venden has illustrated the central dynamics involved in temptation along the following lines: people who drive "wimpy" cars are not tempted to "stomp it." They know that they don't have it "under the hood." People who are most tempted to speed are those who have what we used to refer to as "440 under the hood"! Christ had infinite, divine power "under the hood," and His great temptation was to depend on self rather than the imparted power of the divine Father.

Let's Allow the Balance to Stand!

If Ellen White's finely tuned balance is allowed to stand, her doctrine of Christ's humanity has an appealing wholeness. When one side of the balance is lost sight of or denied, then her thought becomes distorted and can easily be perverted into "believe, only believe" presumption or discouragingly self-centered, behavioristic extremes. Ellen White sought to uphold the delicate balance, and constantly battled the extremes.

In the light of her balanced expression, I would strongly urge that the more traditional expressions such as "pre-Fall" and "post-Fall" are simply insufficient to get at the richness of Ellen White's understanding of Christ's humanity. When it came to Christ as a fully sinless, sacrificial substitute, she was "pre-Fall," but when she spoke of His ability to sustain in times of temptation, she stressed His identity and spoke largely in "post-Fall" terms.

Such a balance certainly involves some aspects of mystery. In fact, I am suggesting the use of such technical words as "balanced tension," "dialectic," or "paradox" to express her profound balance between "sinful" and "sinless" nature. But such expressions of mystery and complexity are not unique to me.

I found it interesting (and comforting) to discover that even writers who argue for the strong *identity*, or the so-called post-Fall position, also want to speak in terms of some tentativeness that evidences a recognition of a mysteriously balanced tension: Gil G. Fernandez speaks of "am biguities" (29), and A. Leroy Moore uses the expression "paradoxical dimensions" (249).

Furthermore, it does not seem to be accidental that their expressions come close to Eric C. Webster (a forceful defender of the sinlessly *uniqueness* position—essentially what the pre-Fall people argue for), who wants to use such terms as *dialectical* (99) and *paradox, tension,* and *antithesis* (152).

It seems that a setting of some mystery and tension, with a balanced use of the terms *uniqueness* and *identity* placed side by side, best expresses her meaning. This allows each concept to make its essential contribution to her very sensible and useful Christology. And the main purpose of this Christology was to serve a practical understanding of salvation, especially the dynamics of sanctification and perfection.

---

[1] This teaching was given its classic expression by (and named after) Arius, a third-century theologian from Alexandria, Egypt.

[2] For further discussion about the theological roots and fruitage of Minneapolis, see chapters 10 and 11.

A Chronological Study

Section 3

JUSTIFICATION BY FAITH

CHAPTER NINE

Justification by Faith—Before 1888

Even though perfection has been the subject of more controversy than has justification, the meaning we give to justification will have a decisive impact on the final definition we give to perfection.

The doctrine of justification by faith is certainly open to distorted interpretations. When Christians talk about "faith alone," the big temptation has usually been to go to some extreme that takes sin lightly and destroys the importance of obedience. But clearly the biblical view is salvation *from* sin, not *in* it. The history of doctrine is full of examples in which this sensible old adage has been sadly neglected.

It is my firm conviction that Ellen White taught a powerfully objective doctrine of justification, but one that does not tolerate willful, premeditated, easy-come-easy-go attitudes toward sin.

Yet if the gospel of justification by faith is taught the way it should be, it may sometimes sound like cheap grace nonsense that makes God's law of none effect. The reason for this seeming perversion is that none of the works of obedience manifest by even "true believers" (Ellen White's term, not Eric Hoffer's) could ever have saving merit.

On the other hand, a balanced teaching of the gospel will also sound like the most demanding forms of perfectionism. The reason for this is that true forgiveness is the key to obedience and all true victory over sin. Receiving God's forgiveness in justification is always accompanied by submission to His Lordship! The fruit of such Lordship will be strict obedience to the Lord's will. Again, we are not saved in sin but from it.

So if you find yourself tempted to accuse me of legalistic perfectionism or to start throwing around such loaded terms as *new theology*, *Fordism*, and *cheap grace*, please hear me out and carefully weigh my evidence from Ellen White on justification by faith.

Justification Before Minneapolis and 1888

As has been pointed out in the first section of this book, Ellen White developed a fairly clear understanding of justification during her sanctification crisis as a teenager. Serious doctrinal reflection on justification in her writings, however, did not begin to manifest itself until the 1870s.

Again it must be emphasized that her understanding before this time was clear that justification was "pardon" and "forgiveness," but it is only with this period that justification begins to receive extended theological clarification and emphasis explicitly essential to Seventh-day Adventism's doctrinal self-understanding.

The most important presentations on justification before Minneapolis came in the addresses that she gave at the 1883 General Conference session in Battle Creek, Michigan, November 9-20. The balance between justification and sanctification had been there from the very beginning of her ministry, but with these addresses this balance tipped the seesaw toward a greater stress on the importance of justification. This sharpening balance became fully expressed in the crisis of 1888 and its aftermath.

Key Elements in Expressing Justification

What were the key elements in her pre-1888 understanding of justification by faith alone? The following were most typical of the way she expressed the doctrine and the experience of it.

Faith and Works Never Separated—Her earliest reflections on justification had more to do with guarding the importance of obedience than projecting a clear concept of objective justification: "Faith will never save you unless it is justified by works" (2T 159; published in 1868). "Faith must be sustained by works; the doers of the work are justified before God" (*ibid.* 167).

Closely related to this prevalent argument against anti-law excuses for disobedience was Ellen White's often-repeated expression that the sinner "can be saved *from* his sins, but not *in* them" (ST, Sept. 4, 1884). This whole concept manifestated Ellen White's clear understanding that faith must always be accompanied by works and that law and gospel are never to be separated, even though their roles are to be clearly distinguished.

One of the most forceful expressions of this close relationship between law and grace, or true faith and obedience, was given in her summation of the experience of John Wesley following his Aldersgate experience: "He continued his strict and self-denying life, not now as the *ground*, but the *result* of faith; not the *root*, but the *fruit* of holiness" (GC 256).

Christian Assurance—In 1870 she declared that believers "should know that we are enjoying the favor of God, that He smiles upon us, and that we are His children indeed . . . [The believer] believes the promise, and it is accounted unto him for righteousness" (RH, Mar. 29, 1870).

It is interesting that this clear statement on the believer's assurance came *before* Ellen White's clearest declarations on justification were preached and penned. Furthermore, this statement is mentioned here to suggest the clarity of Ellen White's pre-1888 understanding of justification.

The discussion of the believer's assurance in Christ was not a prominent theme in her writings, and this immediately raises the question as to why there were so few discussions on this issue.

The reasons for her reticence in this expression appear to be twofold:

1. She perceived serious dangers in the Calvinistic expression of assurance—popularly known as "once saved, always saved." She felt, along with Wesley, that this doctrine was an invitation to presumptuous sinning, causing sinners to think that they were "beyond the reach of temptation" (COL 155).

2. But Ellen White had an even more fundamental objection to saying "I am saved." "Those who accept Christ, and in their first confidence say, I am saved, are in danger of trusting to themselves" (*ibid.*).

In her view, Christian experience has to do with a constant looking away from self and a continuous, conscious dependence on Christ's acceptance and power. Such dependence is based not on how believers feel, but what they know about themselves and about Christ. About themselves, they know they are weak and in constant "need of divine strength" (*ibid.*). About Christ, they know that He loves them and wants them to be saved and that He has the power to do the work they cannot do for themselves (SC 50-55). Certainly such an understanding rules out not only Calvinistic "once saved, always saved" assurance, but also perfectionism.[1]

This concept can perhaps be best illustrated by the old broom-standing-in-the-palm-of-your-hand trick—the moment you take your eyes off the broom head and look at your hand, that moment the broom will fall!

Christ's Merits and Priestly Intercession—The following four concepts are closely related to one another. All have as their common thread the concept of Ellen White's lifelong emphasis on the high priestly intercession of Christ, who was seen to be constantly interceding or advocating for the believers with His own "merit." Furthermore, in the thought of Ellen White, Christ's intercessory ministry is always bound up with His merits. Thus the concept of Christ's merit underlies each of the following points. From 1870 on there was a host of statements to the effect that only the "merits" of Christ could be the basis of salvation, not human works of obedience.

1. Christ's merits make our obedience acceptable. The year 1870 witnessed the first of many expressions of the theme that the "merits" of Christ make the "efforts" of believers "to keep His law" acceptable to God (RH, May 31, 1870). She repeated and developed this theme throughout the coming years into one of her strongest expressions of objective justification (especially after 1888).

This concept was built upon the understanding that all the good works of human beings are polluted with sin and need the objective, accounted merits of Jesus to make them acceptable. And this accounting of sinners as just (or righteous) through Christ's merits was conceived of as constantly necessary all through life! Objective justification is required all the way. "The true follower of Christ" "will see more clearly his own defects, and will feel the need of *continual* repentance, and faith in the blood of Christ"(*ibid.*, Oct. 5, 1886; italics supplied).

This concept is illustrated by a neat looking shirt that appears to be quite clean, but when it is put on, the polluting odor becomes quite apparent—despite the deceptive appearances.

2. Christ's merits make up for our "deficiencies." Closely related to the concept that Jesus is constantly interceding with His "merits" for the sinner were three expressions of the believer's needs that were inextricably bound up with one another. First, as mentioned above, even the good things believers do are polluted by their sinful natures. Second, not only do their sinful natures pollute the good things that they do, but also their performance always involves "deficiencies" and failures. Third, in spite of their sinful natures and deficiencies, however, Christ is willing to intercede, but only for those who have a right attitude toward their sinfulness, "deficiencies," and errors. The dynamic went like this:

Ellen White repeatedly expressed a "high demand" (my words, not hers) understanding of perfect obedience, but there are numerous statements that tend to provide a buffer or safety net against failure to reach the "high demand." Essential to this concept is her teaching that a proper attitude toward Christ and sin on the part of believers makes it possible for Christ to account His righteousness (His "merits") to them despite their deficiencies and failures to meet the high demand.

The picture here is of a high-wire artist who is talented but realistic about the possibility of a slip. The great performer gives it his or her best, but the safety net is always there to catch any failures. The imputed righteousness of Christ is the "safety net" for His faithful but unwittingly faulty children.

"When we have cultivated a spirit of charity, we may commit the keeping of our souls to God as unto a faithful Creator, not because we are sinless, but because Jesus died to save just such erring, faulty creatures as we are. . . . We may rest upon God, not because of our own merit, but because the righteousness of Christ will be imputed to us" (RH, Apr. 22, 1884).

We should carefully note that almost all these buffering or "safety net" statements came after the pioneering presentations on justification at the important 1883 Battle Creek General Conference session.

Could it be that this more forceful expression of justification by faith at Battle Creek tended to heighten Ellen White's appreciation of God's mercy for His failing and deficient children? These safety net statements need to be carefully compared with any similar expressions that follow during the post-1888 era.

3. How Satan's taunting accusations are fended off. In Ellen White's thought, Christ's gracious intercession, with His powerful "merits," certainly placed the Christian on vantage ground. And such vantage ground enables the harried believer to challenge Satan's taunts. The Christian's proper response to the devil's taunting accusations became a favorite vehicle of expression for Ellen White to communicate the believer's acceptance in Jesus. This dramatic expression conjures up visions of a poor, condemned person cowering under the taunts of a pharisaic accuser who has caught her "in the very act." The accused has no defense, only the plea of Christ's merit.

The inspiration for this expression was most likely her exposition of Zechariah 3, the vision of Joshua the high priest. The expression was stated this way: "We cannot answer the charges of Satan against us. Christ alone can make an effectual plea in our behalf" (5T 472). Then she made the justification application clear: "He is able to silence the accuser with arguments founded not upon our merits, but on His own."

This expression has particular importance when placed in the setting of her description of the closing up of the "investigative judgment," the antitypical day of atonement: "Zechariah's vision of Joshua and the Angel applies with peculiar force to the experience of God's people in the closing up of the great day of atonement" (ibid.).

This understanding of the investigative judgment was the occasion to explain further what the proper attitude of the sinful believer should be. She went on to picture God's last people ("the remnant church") as pleading "for pardon and deliverance through Jesus their Advocate. They are fully conscious of the sinfulness of their lives" (ibid. 473). The key issue seemed to be not some antiseptically perfect *performance*, but genuine faith in the Intercessor that begets perfect "*loyalty*."

"The people of God have been in many respects very faulty. . . . But while the followers of Christ have sinned, they have not given themselves to the control of evil. . . .

"They have resisted the wiles of the deceiver; they have not been turned from their loyalty by the dragon's roar" (*ibid.* 474, 475).

Whatever the investigative judgment meant for perfection,[2] it is clear that Ellen White used it to assure God's people that they have One as their high priest who gladly secures "pardon and deliverance," despite the "sinfulness of their lives." With Christ as our advocate, we need not cower before the accusations of the great adversary.

4. God is willing to pardon. While the three preceding points stressed the proper attitude of the believer, this next concept highlighted God's attitude—especially toward the believer.

At the important 1883 Battle Creek General Conference session, Ellen White tried to encourage "many discouraged ones" with the thought that despite "mistakes" that "grieve His Spirit," when sinners "repent, and come to Him with contrite hearts, He will not turn us away" (RH, April 15, 1884). And the penitent ones were encouraged not to wait until they had reformed, but were urged "to come to Him just as we are—sinful, helpless, dependent" (*ibid.*, Apr. 22, 1884).

The imagery here draws heavily on the parable of the prodigal son (which is really the parable of the "prodigious love of the Father"). God is more abundantly willing to receive us than we are to come to Him! The filthy garments permeated with the awful stench and corruption of the pigsty are no obstacle to the Father's redemptive designs!

This imagery was further strengthened at the 1883 Battle Creek General Conference session with the clear warning not to be deceived with the thought that salvation is the result of trusting "partly to God, and partly to themselves."

"While [some] think they are committing themselves to God, there is a great deal of self-dependence. There are conscientious souls that trust partly to God, and partly to themselves. They do not look to God, to be kept by His power, but depend upon watchfulness and the performance of certain duties for acceptance with Him. There are no victories in this kind of faith. . . .

"There is need of constant watchfulness, and of earnest, loving devotion; but these will come naturally when the soul is kept by the power of God through faith. We can do nothing, absolutely nothing, to commend ourselves to divine favor. We must not trust at all to ourselves nor to our good works. . . . God will accept everyone that comes to him trusting wholly in the merits of a crucified Saviour" (1SM 353, 354).

She closed the 1883 General Conference session with a tender expression of God's ready and constant willingness to receive and keep sinners. "The moment you surrender yourself wholly to Him in simple faith, Jesus accepts you, and encircles you in His arms of love. He holds you more firmly than you can grasp Him" (RH, July 22, 1884).

Another interesting expression was the concept that "God's requirement under grace is just the same [as] He made in Eden—perfect obedience to His law." But the strong implication was that the only acceptable obedience to God was Christ's "righteousness" that "is imputed to the obedient." Then the believer was exhorted to "accept it through faith, that the Father shall find in us no sin" (ibid., Sept. 21, 1886).

The scene here is of an Olympic gymnast needing a perfect 10 score but knowing full well that because of a torn ligament he or she is incapable of the 10. But the righteous "judge" imputes it to the gymnast because of a proper attitude, not because of the perfect performance.

Summation

It is very clear that as Ellen White approached the crisis at Minneapolis, she had clearly explained her understanding of justification by faith. While Minneapolis sparked a great emphasis on this doctrine and provoked further clarification of justification as pardon and acceptance, it will not be modified with any concepts which suggest that believers merit salvation because of their obedience.

In the years after 1888 she would explicitly develop the theme implicit in the thought that the merits of Christ, offered in His high priestly intercession, make the best efforts of the believers (defective and feeble though they be) acceptable to God. The central thought in this theme is that Christ's obedient life is accounted to sinners, not just His death.

Let us be very clear about this one. Ellen White taught that our acceptance with Christ is based totally on the merits of His life and death, which are legally, judicially accounted to us. It is not based on His death accounted to us for forgiveness and His life imparted to us so that we can make our own contribution to justification. It is *both* His life and death that justify the penitent believer.

Ellen White's doctrinal independence is here dramatically illustrated in comparison with John Wesley. He was always reluctant to declare Christ's life as accounted to believers, fearful that such a legal accounting might endanger his doctrine of sanctification. He feared that this would open the gates to presumptuous sinning. But this was not the case with Ellen White.

For her, justification by faith was closely related to a proper attitude on the part of believers toward sin, God's requirements, and His merciful attitude toward the faithful. The believer's attitude was declared to be one that involved a desire to obey God and a distaste for sin in any form. (In other words, an attitude of humility as opposed to self-righteousness.) If this attitude of loyalty toward God was evident, then He would safely account sinners as just and righteous, despite their sinful natures, deficiencies, and unwitting failures.

It is impressive that these safety net statements all came after her important expressions of justification at the 1883 General Conference session. Justification is no excuse for sin, but it does provide for the penitent Christ's merits that are a perfect atonement for the failures of the faithful.

---

[1] In this book the term *perfectionist* is not strictly negative but means to have a strong emphasis on God's transforming power. The word "perfectionism" is used only negatively in the sense of believers reaching such a state of perfection that they can no longer be subject to temptation or the possibility of sinning—perfection of nature as opposed to perfection of character.

[2] This theme is addressed in more detail in chapter 6.

CHAPTER TEN

Ministry After Minneapolis— 1888-1902

T his chapter is a continuation of section 1, except it focuses on Ellen White's ministry after 1888. The goal is to describe the historical setting for the important developments during this most critical period of her teaching about salvation.

In this significant 15-year period (1888-1902) we find three important episodes that powerfully shaped the meaning of salvation in Ellen White's ministry: (1) the Minneapolis General Conference session (especially its aftermath), (2) the "Life of Christ" writing project, and (3) the "Receive Ye the Holy Ghost" movement of the latter part of the 1890s and the first two years of the new century.

This remarkable period was certainly the most productive and critical for her writings on salvation during her entire ministry. It was not that there were radically new directions or repudiations of old positions in her understanding, but the years following 1888 witnessed extraordinary emphasis, refinement, and clarification.

Minneapolis and Its Aftermath

This important and controversial conference has stirred heated debate and discussion during the course of the past 100-plus years.

Basically two issues in 1888 complicated the well-known discussion of salvation.

1. For at least two years prior to the 1888 session, there had been a smoldering controversy over the interpretation of Galatians 3:19-25.

The leaders in Battle Creek (led by the president of the General Conference, G. I. Butler, and the revered editor of the *Review*, Uriah Smith) had taken the position that the law in Galatians was the ceremonial law, not the moral law (the Ten Commandments). A group led by E. J. Waggoner (and including W. C. White and A. T. Jones) believed that the "added law" was indeed the moral law.

This was a critical issue for the established ministerial leaders, such as Butler and Smith, who had become able defenders of the authority of the law and the Sabbath. Many Seventh-day Adventist evangelists, following the leadership of Butler and Smith, had been quite successful in defending the law with their position on Galatians against real and perceived opponents of the law.

2. The second issue between the same two groups involved the interpretation of one of the 10 horns of the fourth symbolic beast of Daniel 7. The established General Conference leadership held that this horn symbolized the Huns, but the "progressives" held that the more historically accurate fulfillment was to be found in the Alemanni.

All this must have seemed a bit picky to the observation of non-Seventh-day Adventists during this period, but the atmosphere was such that these issues loomed large in the perspective of the established, older Seventh-day Adventist ministers.

It is probable that the main contributing factor to this charged atmosphere was the heightened sense that something of epic proportions in prophetic fulfillment was about to happen. Movements were under way to make the United States of America a "Christian" nation, and on May 21, 1888, Senator H. W. Blair, of New Hampshire, had just introduced a national Sunday law into Congress. For some years a number of Seventh-day Adventists had been periodically arrested for working on Sunday in different states.

In the view of the Battle Creek leadership, it was no time to be changing interpretations on texts (especially Galatians 3) that might threaten the authority of the moral law with its holy seventh-day Sabbath and prophecies (Daniel 7) that were essential to their mark of the beast interpretations.

This sense of approaching crisis, a sense that Seventh-day Adventism's prophetic interpretations regarding the moral law and the mark of the beast were about to be vindicated in a manifest way, created a strong undercurrent of resistance to younger progressives—Jones, Waggoner, and their West Coast associates. And the established preachers especially targeted Waggoner's presentations on salvation and justification for stiff resistance.

The controversial atmosphere of Minneapolis was further aggravated by personality conflicts and unfortunate conspiracy rumors. These rumors claimed that Ellen White (supposedly influenced by W. C. White, Waggoner, and Jones) was supporting the positions of the young men from the West Coast (1888 Materials 186-189). Such whisperings created a serious crisis of confidence in Ellen White's prophetic authority, especially in the eyes of the Battle Creek leaders.

To further complicate matters, the General Conference session proper was preceded by a 10-day ministerial institute, during which some of these issues were discussed, especially the interpretation of the horns of Daniel 7.

The debate became particularly testy, and this controversial atmosphere carried over from the ministerial institute into the General Conference session proper (Knight 36). Into this troubled setting came E. J. Waggoner as the chief devotional speaker, and he presented his emphasis on righteousness by faith at the General Conference session itself (ibid. 38).

It is not entirely clear what he did present, but whatever it was, it drew a strong, affirmative response from Ellen White, who heartily and publicly endorsed his presentations (much to the dismay of the Battle Creek leaders). And these presentations became the inspiration for the most significant and energetic writing about salvation during Ellen White's entire ministry.

Many questions have arisen among Seventh-day Adventists about the meaning of the 1888 experience, but the primary issue addressed in this book is What did Minneapolis and 1888 mean to Ellen White's ministry and her understanding of salvation? The crucial nature of this question has merited an entire chapter for its full consideration. The answers are not easy to come by, but the evidence is sufficient to clarify the most pressing aspects of this question. More on that in the next chapter. Let us now move on to other important events that shaped her expositions of salvation after Minneapolis.

The "Life of Christ" Project

Ellen White began in earnest her "Life of Christ" project soon after her arrival in Australia in 1892. This project was her major book writing effort during the next eight years and resulted in the publication of her three most important books on the life and teachings of Christ: *Thoughts From the Mount of Blessing* (1896), *The Desire of Ages* (1898), and *Christ's Object Lessons* (1900).

This important enterprise was basically a team effort between Ellen White and her faithful literary assistant Marian Davis. Ms Davis' work was to search through previous writings (letters, periodical articles, and books) for appropriate material. She would then paste them up in "blank books." She organized this material, and when she would find a subject or narrative from the life of Christ not adequately covered, Ellen White "would fill in the gaps" (ALW, *Ellen G. White: The Australian Years* 383).

For the purposes of this study, two things need to be pointed out. First, because of Ms. Davis' gleaning work in previous writings, much of the material was not new. Second, most of the material of significance on salvation referred mainly to sanctification, putting great emphasis on character perfection. Justification was dwelt upon, but compared with sanctification and perfection, it was a minor theme as far as space and intensity of expression were concerned.

These facts raise three questions related to the concerns of the balance of this section: 1. Were there any new developments in her understanding of perfection manifested during this period? 2. What would account for the dominance of perfectionist materials during this time? 3. Did this perfectionist emphasis in any way modify her powerful emphasis and expression of justification found in the years immediately following 1888?

"Receive Ye the Holy Ghost"

The last half of the 1890s witnessed a remarkable perfectionist movement that involved many of the church's most sought after revival speakers. Knight refers to this revival as "The Adventist Holiness Movement" (167).

This crusade certainly had its main origins in the revival preaching and writing of A. T. Jones. Its proponents saw it as the climax of the Minneapolis righteousness by faith emphasis. It also was a conscious development in Seventh-day Adventism that was directly influenced by the broader Holiness movement of the late nineteenth century and its fledgling child the early Pentecostal movement (Knight 167-170; Schwarz 447). The major leaders, aside from Jones, were A. F. Ballenger, E. J. Waggoner, and Mrs. S.M.I. Henry.

The perfectionistic tone of the movement was evident in Jones' preaching by 1895, as he was preaching "translation faith" and "the power to overcome every tendency to sin" (Knight 170). A. F. Ballenger echoed these same sentiments as he proclaimed that righteousness by faith "was given us of God to stop our sinning. Let no man say that he has received righteousness by faith until he has stopped sinning."

This emphasis was related to the Holy Ghost theme, with the added declaration that "we are in the time of the latter rain, but the outpouring of the Spirit is withheld because of our sins." Personal holiness, however, was not the only object of this revival, as Ballenger proclaimed that this "baptism of the Holy Spirit" would "furnish . . . mighty power to" witness to "the world" (Haloviak, "Pioneers" 4).

In 1897 A. T. Jones added the "significant ingredient" that "perfect holiness embraces the flesh as well as the spirit; it includes the body as well as the soul" (ibid.). Thus "health reform with the indwelling of the Holy Spirit was consistently emphasized in the Review between 1897 and 1900" (ibid.).

This was not, however, just preventive health reform, which had been consistently emphasized by Seventh-day Adventist health advocates. The "Holy Ghost" preachers also included faith healing. Ballenger promoted "physical healing" as "now present truth to Seventh-day Adventists" (*ibid.* 4).

Haloviak points out that Ballenger's "theological base" for "physical healing" was his concept of the atonement, which included "more than Christ bearing the sins of the world in its behalf. It included, for Ballenger, Christ bearing the physical illnesses of the world upon the cross." Ballenger "reasoned that it required no greater miracle for God to save him from sins and keep him from falling than to heal physical ills." He then went on to stress "that anyone who could believe in the resurrection of the body could readily believe in the healing of the body" (*ibid.* 5).

The whole message certainly involved a very close brush with a concept that viewed God as mystically diffused throughout His universe. Already there were hints of pantheistic elements, which would later contribute to numerous prominent defections from the Seventh-day Adventist Church.

The "Receive Ye the Holy Ghost" message was the popular expression of this mystical view of God. Philosophical pantheism (advocated most notably by Kellogg) was the more sophisticated version. But these two strands were closely connected, as both Jones and Waggoner harbored strong pantheistic tendencies along with their popular participation in the "Holy Ghost" movement (Knight 171).

Knight suggests that such mystical concepts were further accented in "the teaching of Jones, Waggoner, and [W. W.] Prescott on righteousness by faith" in that "they often overly literalized the Bible's teaching on the indwelling of the Holy Spirit" (*ibid.* 171).

The most spectacular manifestation of the "Receive Ye the Holy Ghost" movement was the "Holy Flesh" fanaticism in Indiana. Though Jones later repudiated this movement, it is clear that his preaching (along with Ballenger's) was one of the key sources of this manifestation of "Adventist Pentecostalism" (*ibid.* 169).

Indiana and "Holy Flesh"

Under the leadership of R. S. Donnell (the conference president) and S. S. Davis (the conference revivalist), the "Holy Ghost" movement in Indiana advocated an emotional experience in which "both the mind and the body were fully cleansed and brought back to the condition of man before the fall, 'so far as its life or actions are concerned'" (Haloviak, "Pioneers" 10).

Richard W. Schwarz reports that this sinless condition was achieved in an atmosphere in which "individuals frequently fell prostrate. . . . Once a stricken member revived, he was declared to have passed 'through the garden experience' which Christ had in Gethsemane. This experience demonstrated that a person was a 'born' son of God, fully cleansed from sin and sinful tendencies and released from the power of death; he was now ready for translation. Those who did not have the 'garden experience' might still be saved, but as 'adopted' sons of God they would have to go 'to heaven on the underground railroad'—that is, they must die first" (447).

As the 1890s progressed, there was a noticeable increase in emphasis on the person and work of the Holy Spirit in the writings of Ellen White, but the excitable perfectionism of the holy flesh movement was too extreme. This manifestation of Adventist Holiness-Pentecostalism was soundly, personally, and publicly rebuked by the prophet in a very pointed testimony given at the 1901 General Conference session in Battle Creek, Michigan: "All may now obtain holy hearts, but it is not correct to claim in this life to have holy flesh. . . .

"If those who speak so freely of perfection in the flesh could see things in the true light, they would recoil with horror from their presumptuous ideas. . . .

"While we cannot claim perfection of the flesh, we may have Christian perfection of the soul. Through the sacrifice made in our behalf, sins may be perfectly forgiven" (2SM 32).

It is interesting that when Ellen White was confronted with a serious variety of Holiness fanaticism, she instinctively embraced a more justificationist response. The entire testimony given at the 1901 session, rebuking the holy flesh advocates, was filled with concepts of perfection through the blood of Christ that cleanses and frees the "conscience . . . from condemnation" (ibid. 32).

We should note here, consistent with the years previous to 1888, that almost all Ellen White's references to Holiness teachings from 1889 to 1902 were negative. She consistently perceived Holiness teachings to be undermining the authority of God's law, extremely emotional, and bitterly opposed to the distinctives of Seventh-day Adventism.

For Ellen White, holiness and perfection continue to receive great emphasis, but holiness teachings and experience must always have the following characteristics: (1) They must not be excessively emotional; (2) they must always involve an understanding of objective justification by faith alone in the grace and merits of Jesus; (3) they must always be presented and promoted in the setting of Seventh-day Adventism's distinctive teachings; (4) they can involve perfection of "character" (though not instantaneously), but not of "flesh" or "nature" until glorification; and (5) it must always involve sober obedience to the Ten Commandments.

Summation

Through all the years, whether justification or sanctification was getting the accent or emphasis in her ministry, Ellen White always sought balance in her presentations. But for our purposes in this section, the most pressing question is How did Minneapolis affect her presentations on justification? It is to this question that we next turn.

CHAPTER ELEVEN

The Significance and Meaning of Minneapolis and 1888

Because of the controverted nature of the meaning of Minneapolis, I feel that a separate chapter is needed to present evidence for what this momentous General Conference session meant to Ellen White and her ministry. I know that volumes have been devoted to this subject, but I ask the reader to indulge me this review, because it is crucial if we are to get a clear grasp of Ellen White's balanced view of salvation.

For Ellen White, Minneapolis was not primarily about perfection, better relations among ministers, points of prophetic interpretation, or even the nature of Christ's humanity. Minneapolis was primarily a great turning point in the intensity and further clarity of her expressions of justification by faith.

But once again I must emphasize that there were no major reversals of her previous teaching. It is not that she came to Minneapolis and admitted to the assembled brethren that she had been tragically legalistic in her ministry for the previous 45 years. To the contrary, she claimed to have preached the "matchless charms of Christ" all those years. But she did say that there was an urgent need to uplift (for special consideration) the subject of justification by faith in Christ's saving merits. This subject needed special attention not only because of the spiritual needs of God's people but also because of doctrinal confusion as to the real meaning of justification by faith.

I realize that this interpretation is a conclusion about 1888 that has not had wide support. Therefore it behooves one to present some rather compelling evidence to sustain a position that flies in the face of long-held, seemingly established interpretations. What is the evidence that in Ellen White's thinking Minneapolis was primarily about justification?

Ellen White and 1888

What did Minneapolis mean to Ellen White? The answer to this question is not easy to find. Two further questions arise at this juncture: 1. Is Ellen White's reaction to Minneapolis to be judged by the more immediate impact it had on her preaching and writing, or by the way it affected her thinking during the balance of her career? 2. What was her relationship to the views and teachings of Jones and Waggoner?

The Long or the Short View of 1888?—As becomes evident in this study, the 1890s presented two major emphases: the strong accent on justification in the three to four years immediately following 1888, and the strong emphasis on perfection during the last half of the 1890s. Which is the "1888 Ellen White"?

It should already be abundantly evident that Ellen White did not want to deny either side of the justification-sanctification balance. It is also clear from her own writings that she commented on the Minneapolis crisis for the rest of her life.

When all factors are considered, however, the bulk of the evidence strongly suggests that the main message of Minneapolis had special application to the immediate aftermath of the conference—the following three years of her ministry before her departure for Australia. It is quite evident that Ellen White saw the church in a great crisis. This crisis had its roots in both doctrinal misconceptions about justification and an obvious failure to experience what the doctrine sought to describe.

As becomes abundantly clear in succeeding sections of this chapter, the immediate impact of Minneapolis on Ellen White resulted in the most intense period of emphasis on justification by faith in her entire career.

Following Minneapolis, Ellen White never denied the high goals of sanctification and perfection. But the major theme of her ministry was a message to the church that believers were to quit trying to merit salvation by good works and obedience to the law and accept the wonderful forgiveness of Jesus that "is made manifest in obedience to all the commandments of God."

She would go on to contend that "many had lost sight of Jesus. They needed to have their eyes directed to His divine person, His merits, and His changeless love for the human family" (TM 92).

Doctrinal Confusion Over Justification—There was definite doctrinal confusion about salvation that had led to a period of spiritual dryness and unintentional legalistic discouragement. The problem clearly involved doctrinal dispute, not just deficiencies in personal Christian experience.

This understanding, I recognize, goes against some of the conclusions of R. J. Wieland, one of the major interpreters of Minneapolis. Wieland declares that the issues of 1888 were certainly doctrinal, but the evidence, as I read it, suggests that he identifies the wrong doctrines. While he has acknowledged that justification was a major emphasis, the thesis that receives his major accent seems to go like this: 1888 represented a great emphasis on the truth that Jesus had a sinful nature, just like fallen humanity, and this deep identity with sinners enables them to reproduce His character in a profound experience of sanctification (Wieland, *Introduction* 19-54). Such a position might be attributed to Jones and Waggoner, but this was not what 1888 moved Ellen White to emphasize.

Wieland's position on the nature of Christ as a central emphasis of 1888 is seriously undermined by the very stubborn fact that in all the *1888 Materials* recently published by the Ellen G. White Estate, only three or four isolated references to the nature of Christ can be found. George Knight is right on target when he contends that none of the records of Minneapolis "demonstrate that the divinity of Christ, the human nature of Christ, or 'sinless living' were topics of emphasis or discussion at the 1888 meetings. Persons holding that those topics were central to the theology of the meetings generally read subsequent developments in Jones and Waggoner's treatment of righteousness by faith back into the 1888 meetings" (Knight 37).

In essence it appears that the positions of Wieland and his admirers have missed the central point of the whole 1888 emphasis—making sanctification and the nature of Christ the major thrusts, rather than justification.

1888, Jones and Waggoner, and Ellen White—Regarding the question of her relationship to the ministry of Jones and Waggoner, it is also interesting that Wieland and Short contend that the 1888 message is what Jones and Waggoner defined it to be (not Ellen White). But they then go to great pains to seek to prove that Ellen White was in full agreement with Jones and Waggoner (Wieland and Short 63).

The question then becomes Did Ellen White agree with Jones and Waggoner enough on the issues of 1888 so that it can be said that they were in substantial agreement?

Ellen White's hearty support of Jones and Waggoner is unquestioned. The key issue, however, seems to be whether this strong support meant *total* support for all their theological positions. For instance, did she support their view that Christ was a created god (Arianism)? Did her support of Waggoner mean that she agreed with his later views on "spiritual affinities," a doctrine which taught that one could have a "spiritual" relationship to someone not his or her spouse, but be married to that person in heaven? I think the answer is obvious.

But it might be argued that it was her support of their views on salvation that was clear, not these other issues. Even here, however, it is evident that her support was not some sort of blank check (Knight 72). Ellen White was indisputably clear when she told the delegates assembled at Minneapolis that "some interpretations of Scripture, given by Dr. Waggoner, I do not regard as correct" (MS 15, 1888, in Knight 72). Fifteen months later she declared: "Without a doubt . . . God has given precious truth at the right time to Bro. Jones and Bro. Waggoner. Do I place them as infallible? Do I say that they will not make a statement, nor have an idea that cannot be questioned? or that cannot be error? Do I say so? No, I do not say any such thing" (MS 56, 1890, in Knight 72).

It thus clearly becomes an open question whether she held similar views on perfection and Christ's humanity. One cannot simply say, "Ellen White gave great and extended endorsement to Jones and Waggoner, and thus everything that they said on the nature of Christ, justification, and perfection was her position and the infallible message of the Holy Spirit!"

Again, it must be emphasized that the central concern of this study is *What did 1888 mean to Ellen White's understanding of salvation (not to Jones and Waggoner's)?*

In the entire scope of Ellen White's ministry, the nature of Christ and sanctification were of central importance, but the urgent need of Seventh-day Adventists in 1888 (and its immediate aftermath) was to understand that they were accepted by faith in the accounted merits of Christ—and not because of their good works. Only as they shed this un-witting legalism (and its false doctrinal basis) could they make any significant progress in the life of holiness and perfection.

The Experiential Interpretation of 1888—On the other hand, some have contended that the "main issues in the 1888 righteousness by faith meetings were not doctrinal but experiential" (Knight 65). These interpreters seem to be following in the wake of A. G. Daniells' interpretation of 1888 (in *Christ Our Righteousness*).

Daniells, a longtime associate of Ellen White's and a former General Conference president, claimed that "the essence of Ellen White's concern regarding 1888" "was not doctrinal but experiential" (Knight 67; Daniells 21, 11). This position is demonstrably not supported by the primary documents of Ellen White during the three or four years immediately following 1888.

It is abundantly clear that Seventh-day Adventist ministers were not conducting their doctrinal discussions in a very charitable spirit, and there was an apparent need for a deeper level of spirituality to be manifested in their ministry as a whole. But this did not deny Ellen White's forcefully insistent call for doctrinal clarification, especially on objective justification.

For Ellen White there was undoubtedly more involved than the mere "subjective application of an undisputed doctrine" (Haloviak, "Review of Knight" 24). There was important doctrinal dispute, and she was a disputant, albeit one who called for charitable discussion.

Ellen White: The Unique Champion of Justification?—Further evidence that there was doctrinal confusion in the church was Ellen White's declaration that what Waggoner presented at Minneapolis "was the first clear teaching on this subject from any human lips I had heard, excepting the conversations between myself and my husband" (*1888 Materials* 349). Was she the only person in Seventh-day Adventism who had had a clear conception of justification by faith?

Careful research by Bert Haloviak has not been able to uncover anything in Adventism before 1888 that came close to Ellen White's clear teaching of objective justification, and he has concluded that she was indeed the unique champion of objective justification in Adventism before 1888.[1]

Consistent with the evidence presented in successive sections of this chapter, Haloviak persuasively contends that "Christ's work as mediator is always implicit in Ellen White's concept of acceptable obedience. Christ's mediation makes our imperfect, but sincere, works acceptable. It is here where Ellen White far transcended the theological system of both the pioneers[2] and Jones and Waggoner" ("From Righteousness to Holy Flesh: Judgment at Minneapolis," 23).

The evidence thus strongly suggests that the crisis of 1888 definitely involved doctrinal confusion on subjects that had to do with salvation—especially justification. And Ellen White would spend the next three years in extensive travels, seeking to clarify the issues of Minneapolis.

The Four Years After 1888

The clarity and intensity of her expression on justification was evident in a number of striking ways. The rest of this chapter will seek to document this remarkable emphasis on justification by faith. It will also demonstrate not only her efforts to relieve the arid spiritual conditions in dry hills of the Adventist Gilboa, but also her attempts to clear up doctrinal confusion.

The Great Mass of Material on Justification— Of the body of material on justification by faith gathered for this book (what she wrote from 1844 to 1902), roughly *45 percent of the entire mass was recorded between December 1888 and December 1892.* Let that sink in for a moment! In other words, nearly half of all her writings on this aspect of salvation was recorded in one four-year span of a 58-year ministry (1844-1902).

Think of it this way. What if you had a pastor for four years in your church and nearly half the sermons he preached during that time were on justification? Would you not remember this preacher as the "justification by faith" pastor?

Furthermore, this astonishing mass of material on justification came forth from her pen and preaching with constant regularity during this entire, critical four-year period—not just the few months after November 1888.

Strenuous Preaching Tours in Support of Justification—Her travels during the three years between Minneapolis and her departure for Australia were largely given to tours around the United States in support of a clearer understanding of justification by faith and a deeper experience of the love and acceptance of God. Approximately the first year and a half after Minneapolis were particularly intense (ALW, *Ellen G. White: The Lonely Years* 417, 418).

In just about every meeting she attended across North America, her burden was pardon through faith in Christ's imputed merits. Note the impressive sampling that follows.

Battle Creek, Michigan, December 8-22, 1888. During a sermon she urged the people to "plead the blood of a crucified and risen Saviour by living faith, that pardon may be written opposite our names" (RH, Dec. 18, 1888).

South Lancaster, Massachusetts, January 11-19, 1889. After exhorting the people on the "necessity of obeying the law of God," she went on to observe that "many, even among the ministers" were understanding the truth "as it is in Jesus in a light in which they had never before viewed it." Jesus was seen to be "a sin-pardoning Saviour." Many were struggling with the idea that they had a "great work to do themselves before they can come to Christ," thinking "that Jesus will come in at the very last of their struggle, and give them help by putting the finishing touch to their life-work."

Ottawa, Kansas, May 7-28, 1889. In a sermon preached to the ministers of the Kansas Conference she defined "belief" as fully accepting "that Jesus Christ died as our sacrifice; that He became the curse for us, took our sins upon Himself, and imputed unto us His own righteousness" (FW 63-79).

In a report of the camp meeting that followed the ministers' meeting, she told of "light" flashing "from the oracles of God in relation to the law and the gospel, in relation to the fact that Christ is our righteousness." That this was *not primarily sanctifying righteousness* was made clear when she spoke of one of the "young ministering brethren" who testified that "he had enjoyed more of the blessing and love of God during that meeting than in all his life before. . . . He saw that it was his privilege to be justified by faith; he had peace with God, and with tears confessed what relief and blessing had come to his soul."

Ellen White sensed a large, collective sigh of relief spontaneously coming forth from Seventh-day Adventist souls as they received the "tidings that Christ is our righteousness" (RH, July 23, 1889).

This same theme runs through the sermons and reports of numerous other camp meetings, the 1889 General Conference Session, and the important Bible School for ministers held in Battle Creek during the first half of 1890 (ALW, *Ellen G. White: The Lonely Years:* 453).

Seventh-day Adventism was alive with interest in the subject of "justification by faith." Ellen White was uniting her efforts with Jones and Waggoner in strenuous tours to promote the good news of the sin-pardoning Saviour. While these tours began to slacken in 1890, the basic theme of justification continued to find forceful expression in her writings (published and unpublished) until her departure for Australia in late 1891.

"The Matchless Charms of Christ"—Ellen White declared that the ideas which Waggoner presented at Minneapolis were "the first clear teaching on this subject from any human lips I had heard, excepting the conversations between myself and my husband."

There is good evidence for the truthfulness of her claim, especially among Seventh-day Adventist leaders. But what is not clear from her testimonies about 1888 were her time references—what she meant when she declared that what she had been "presenting" to the people "for the *last 45 years*" (italics supplied) was "the matchless charms of Christ"—a clear reference to Waggoner's presentations on justification at Minneapolis (*1888 Materials* 348, 349).

It is obvious that she had understood justification by faith from her early days and that during the 15 or so years previous to Minneapolis she did present some excellent material on justification. But I was hard-pressed to find such an accent on objective justification in the time frame of "the last 45 years" to which she referred. This is especially evident when compared to what she began presenting in the late 1870s, the 1883 General Conference session presentations, and the flood of material that came after 1888.

She felt she had uplifted Christ, and certainly the statement which declared that "for years" "the matter has been kept so constantly urged upon me" (*ibid.* 810) has more special reference to the 1883-1890 period. In the light of this statement, what is to be made of the claim that she had emphasized justification since the beginning of her ministry?

Some might suggest that she was simply given to exaggeration in her claim. But a better explanation seems to go more along the following lines.

First, we need to recognize that an explicitly doctrinal reference to justification by faith (using technical terms such as *justification* and *imputation*) is almost impossible to find before 1868. But what she seemed to have had in mind in claiming to present "the matchless charms of Christ" "for the last 45 years" was her *overall Christ-centered ministry*.

Undoubtedly she was referring to the sum total of her doctrinal and spiritual impact, *not just the technical precision of her theological expression on justification*.

Even in her early ministry she often spoke of pardon and forgiveness, expressions of justification that were less theological than such terms as *imputation* and *justification*. Haloviak is helpful at this point: "It should be observed that Ellen White did not present the points alluded to (objective justification) in a conscious theological manner. . . . Her conclusions seemed to spring from an objective view of Christ that she maintained from the earliest days of her ministry" (Haloviak, "From Righteousness to Holy Flesh: Judgment at Minneapolis," 5:6, 7).

This concept of an "objective view of Christ" advocating for us as our high priestly mediator was explicit in Adventist theology from the very beginning. But among Seventh-day Adventists it appears that only Ellen White was exploiting its possibilities to the fullest for the expression of objective justification.

What is most striking about these testimonies to her past, professedly unique understanding of justification (among Seventh-day Adventists) is that they were all in the immediate aftermath of 1888. Nothing like them is found in any other period of her ministry. Minneapolis was certainly an inspiration to a great call for Christ-centered ministry in the setting of justification by faith.

"*Let the Law Take Care of Itself*"—The charge that this great emphasis on justification by faith would destroy the authority of God's law was particularly intense during the early months of 1890. This probably arose from the presentations that were being made at the lengthy "Bible School" in Battle Creek that had been called to promote the understanding of justification by faith. It was quite likely that most of these charges were generated by such persons as Uriah Smith and his supporters, who had been the main opposers of Jones and Waggoner (and, more subtly, of Ellen White) at Minneapolis and afterward.

It is significant that Ellen White (no mean defender of the law herself) was not deterred by such suspicions of anti-law sentiments. It was in this context that she made her startling challenge to the law partisans to "let the law take care of itself. We have been at work on the law until we get as dry as the hills of Gilboa. . . . Let us trust in the merits of Jesus" (*1888 Materials* 557).

She went on to amplify this response: "Some of our brethren have expressed fears that we shall dwell too much upon the subject of justification by faith, but I hope and pray that none will be needlessly alarmed; for there is no danger in presenting this doctrine as it is set forth in the Scriptures. If there had not been a remissness in the past to properly instruct the people of God, there would not now be a necessity of calling especial attention to it. . . .

"Several have written to me, inquiring if the message of justification by faith is the third angel's message, and I have answered, 'It is the third angel's message in verity'" (1SM 372).

To many Seventh-day Adventists, especially the partisans of the Battle Creek establishment preachers, these words must have seemed rather shocking. But Ellen White was not to be deterred. She kept moving ahead in her strong advocacy of justification with the bold declaration that she "could see no cause for alarm" and that "this fear [of destroying the law] was cherished by those who had not heard all the lessons given." She continued: "Many remarks have been made to the effect that in our camp meetings the speakers have dwelt upon the law, the law, and not on Jesus. This statement is not strictly true, but have not the people had some reason for making these remarks?" (1888 Materials 890, 891).

This strong denial that justification by faith would downgrade God's law is potent evidence of the forcefulness with which she and others were promoting justification in this period immediately following Minneapolis.

As was noted at the beginning of this section on justification, when the gospel is preached in all its power, it will sometimes sound like an attack on the law and true obedience. But for Ellen White it really was not an attack on the law. For her, in the legalistic setting of late nineteenth-century Adventism, it was an attack on the misuse of the law as a means of gaining merit for salvation.

Summation

Ellen White can never be accused of improperly downgrading the essential importance of sanctification, perfection, and character transformation. She can in no wise be charged with doing away with the authority of God's law and the redeemed person's obligation to obey it in grace. But there is abundant evidence that the great need of God's people during the years around 1888 was a clearer understanding of the much neglected subject of justification by faith.

For Ellen White, Minneapolis was a great incentive to uplift Christ as the sin-pardoning Redeemer. She did not denigrate subjects related to obedience. But she clearly sounded a clarion note that God's people will not be able to move forward in their Christian experience unless they have a clear view of the assurance of His marvelous acceptance through Christ's justifying merits.

---

[1] This conclusion has been reached by Haloviak in "From Righteousness to Holy Flesh: Judgment at Minneapolis." His presentation in chapter 5 is especially informative.

[2] Here Haloviak uses the term *pioneers* to refer to the established ministers at Battle Creek headquarters—especially Uriah Smith and G. I. Butler.

CHAPTER 12

Justification After Minneapolis —From Late 1888 to 1892

The comparison of Ellen White's post-Minneapolis periods with her pre-Minneapolis conceptions of justification is best demonstrated by comparing the major expressions or categories used in chapter 9 with how they unfolded during each of the periods of the post-Minneapolis era. Any additions to these three essential expressions will be noted as the study unfolds.

Faith and Works Never Separated

The close relationship between law and gospel, faith and works, and the expression that sinners are saved *from* sin, not *in* sin, continued with undiminished force during this critical period that saw Ellen White's most vigorous explanations of justification.

The balance between justification and sanctification that had been in her understanding from the earliest days was not denied or modified, even though the justification side was now receiving its most forceful expression. There were no marked changes in her basic doctrine from the previous era, and such a lack of change is strong evidence of the central importance of the justification/sanctification balance in the salvation teachings of Ellen White.

The quartet of ideas growing out of her emphasis on the high priestly intercession of Christ unfolded in the following manner.

Christ's Merits Make Our Obedience Acceptable—The expression that the "merits" of Christ make the "efforts" of believers "to keep His law" acceptable to God is not only repeated but also clarified to give an even stronger statement of objective justification. She not only spoke of Christ's "merits" making their efforts acceptable, but she explicitly called these "merits" "His perfection."

"When He sees men lifting the burdens, trying to carry them in lowliness of mind, with distrust of self and with reliance upon Him," the sinner's "defects are covered by the perfection and fullness of the Lord our righteousness." Such humble believers are "looked upon by the Father with pitying, tender love; He regards such as obedient children, and the righteousness of Christ is imputed unto them" (1888 Materials 402; IHP 23).

In the important manuscript 36, 1890, Ellen White used the strong expression "creature merit" and spoke of its "utter worthlessness . . . to earn the wages of eternal life." It is not entirely clear from the context if this refers to the believer's present efforts (not just the preconversion efforts of the well-meaning but misguided penitent to win God's favor), but the strong implication is that this was what she had in mind. She referred to "a fervor of labor and an intense affection, high and noble achievement of intellect, a breadth of understanding, and the humblest self-abasement" (FW 23) as needing to "be laid upon the fire of Christ's righteousness to cleanse it from its earthly odor before it rises in a cloud of fragrant incense to the great Jehovah and is accepted as a sweet savor" (ibid. 24). She then reinforced the need for Christ's intercessory ministry (and the implication that it was the converted believer's righteousness that was in vogue here) with the declaration that "my requests are made acceptable only because they are laid upon Christ's righteousness"(ibid.).

The notion that it is the believer's prayers for the forgiveness of sin that need intercession, however, became explicit in 1892. "But suppose that we sin after we have been forgiven, after we have become the children of God, then need we despair? No; for John writes, 'My little children, these things I write unto you, that ye sin not. And if any man sin, we have an advocate with the Father, Jesus Christ the righteous.' Jesus is in the heavenly courts pleading with the Father in our behalf. He presents our prayers, mingling with them the precious incense of His own merit, that our prayers may be acceptable to the Father" (RH, Mar. 1, 1892). It was clearly stated that whatever believers do—even their best works—is in need of the objective ministry of Christ's intercession to make their works acceptable.

The picture that she portrayed here is probably the most arresting depiction of objective justification Ellen White would ever give. She pictures sinners as outwardly doing the right things, but their actions are in desperate need of Christ's precious incense—"His own merit." This justification is objective in that its power depends on what Christ does in heaven, not what goes on subjectively in the believer. What goes on in the believer is good, but not good enough!

This most powerful portrayal would continue to receive further expression (and some elaboration) through 1902.

Christ's Merits Make Up for Our "Deficiencies"—Already in the immediately preceding section, we have clear examples of what I call her safety net expressions: even if believers "sin" after having been forgiven, they have their prayers for forgiveness perfumed with the "fragrance" of the "incense of His own merit." Please note that these "merits" are to be contrasted with "creature merit" of sinful humans. With the power of Christ's merits being offered to the sinful (by nature), deficient, sinning, but penitent and loyal children of God, they have their "unavoidable deficiencies" made up for them by the "imputed" righteousness of Christ (3SM 195-197).

Again, during this period, both of the closely related themes of "deficiencies" that need to be made up for and the forgiveness of sins committed by erring believers (but erring ones who are loyal and trying to obey) continued to receive ongoing expression. The strength of the expression, however, was increased with the declaration that these deficiencies are "unavoidable," a qualifying term not found in pre-1888 materials. Furthermore, she referred to the "merits" that humans would seek to produce not just as "merit" but clarified this with the more strikingly negative expression "creature merit."

The expression "unavoidable deficiencies" cries out for further comment. She strengthened this expression with a number of other striking terms and phrases.*

"His perfect holiness atones for our *shortcomings*. When we do our best, He becomes our righteousness" (*1888 Materials* 242).

"The sinner's *defects* are covered by the perfection and fullness of the Lord our Righteousness," and they are regarded as "obedient children" (*ibid.* 402; IHP 23).

"When we are clothed with the righteousness of Christ, we shall have no relish for sin." Such believers "*may make mistakes*," but they will "hate *the sin* that caused the sufferings of the Son of God" (RH, March 18, 1890).

"The sinner *may err*, but he is not cast off without mercy" (*1888 Materials* 898).

"If through manifold temptations we *are surprised or deceived into sin*, he does not turn from us, and leave us to perish. No, no, that is not like our Saviour" (RH, Sept. 1, 1891).

"Jesus loves His children, *even if they err*. . . . He keeps His eye upon them, and when they do their best . . . be assured the service will be accepted, *although imperfect*" (3SM 195, 196).

"*We make mistakes again and again*," and "*no one is perfect but Jesus. . . . What if in some respects we do err*, does the Lord forsake us, and forget us, and leave us to our own ways? No" (*1888 Materials* 1089).

The collective force of these expressions certainly envisions a reassuring safety net in light of the reality of human failure. It is an unmistakably powerful expression of objective justification. While this exposition was essentially the same as during the previous era, the combined effect does seem stronger and more comprehensive in this period (at least in the number of times expressed).

Especially the phrases "unavoidable deficiencies" and "no one is perfect but Jesus" clearly provide a softening buffer against the failure to meet the "high demand" and must be seriously considered in any final definition of what Ellen White meant by "perfection."

Fending Off Satan's Taunting Accusations—The rather dramatic expression of dialogue between the harassed sinner and the taunting devil continued to manifest itself. A direct reference to the vision of Joshua and the angel of Zechariah 3 was a marked application of the justificationist buffering against human failure. "Jesus is perfect. Christ's righteousness is imputed unto them, and He will say, 'Take away the filthy garments from him and clothe him with change of raiment.' Jesus makes up for our unavoidable deficiencies" (3SM 196).

Please note that this use of Zechariah 3 was employed in the same context as the important expression that Christ's imputed righteousness makes up for "our unavoidable deficiencies." Furthermore, this dramatic dialogue was placed at least twice in the context of Jesus' ministry in the Most Holy Place. In the thought of Ellen White, the ministry of Christ in the Most Holy Place was intimately related to the proceedings connected with the "investigative judgment."

"Satan will accuse you of being a great sinner, and you must admit this, but you can say: 'I know I am a sinner, and that is the reason I need a Saviour.' Jesus came into the world to save sinners" (ST, July 4, 1892).

Four paragraphs later in the same article she declared: "Jesus stands in the holy of holies, now to appear in the presence of God for us. There He ceases not to present His people moment by moment, complete in Himself."

This *Signs* article, along with manuscript 36, 1890, ranks as one of the most powerful and comprehensive expressions of objective justification, by faith alone, in all Ellen White's writings.

This statement certainly presents the work of Christ in the Most Holy Place as having to do with objective justification, a justification that must be constantly ministered to His defective people, who are presented "moment by moment" as "complete in Himself."

But a second statement that spoke to this theme during this period was an even more explicit reference to the work of Christ in the "judgment" and is found in manuscript 40, 1891: "The Lord has promised that because of the propitiatory sacrifice He will, if we repent, certainly forgive our iniquities. Now, while Christ is pleading in our behalf, while the Father accepts the merits of the atoning Sacrifice, let us ask and we shall receive. Let all confess their sins and let them go beforehand to judgment that they may be forgiven for Christ's sake, and that pardon may be written against their names. . . .

"With Jesus as your Advocate, and you believing, confessing your sins with contrition of soul, and dying to self, would you not feel assured your suit is indeed gained?" (*1888 Materials* 868, 869).

The implications for justification in the way she employed the concept of the investigative judgment continued the same trends as found in the previous era. The judgment not only motivated character transformation, but did so by giving assurance that the faithful could find acceptance in Christ.

God's Willingness to Pardon—The expression of God's willingness to pardon continued in much the same fashion as found in the previous era, with no marked development.

The sum total of these four critical expressions which have to do with Christ's intercessory ministry was that objective justification is needed by believers all the way through their experience. Justification always runs parallel to or concurrently with sanctification.

It is absolutely clear that believers must always be looking to Jesus for their merits. There is neither a time nor a place in our Christian experience that we can begin to look to self. Such an experience is best illustrated by the electric trolley car compared with the bus.

The trolley gets down the street by keeping its boom connected to the source of power from above. The bus gets along by depending on the power it receives from its own fuel tanks. The simple fact is that believers simply do not have enough in the "tank" to make it when it comes to merit. We must be trolley cars all the way to the kingdom—every moment and mile of the way!

God's Infinite Requirements Necessitate Justification

The concept that God's requirement is now just what it was in Eden before the Fall was expressed very clearly in justificationist terms. Ellen White used two such expressions during this period.

The first came in *Steps to Christ*. Because "we are sinful, unholy, we cannot perfectly obey the holy law." But despite past sinfulness sinners can be "accounted righteous. Christ's character stands in place of your character, and you are accepted before God just as if you had not sinned" (62).

Although this application seems to have primary reference to justification, Ellen White did express her justification/sanctification balance with the thought that God works in sinners so that "with Christ working in you, you will manifest the same spirit and do the same good works— works of righteousness, obedience.

"So we have nothing in ourselves of which to boast. We have no ground for self-exaltation. Our only ground of hope is in the righteousness of Christ imputed to us, and in that wrought by His Spirit working in and through us" (ibid. 63).

There was here the hint that what God does in believers can, based on a clear experience of Christ's imputed righteousness, produce "the same spirit and do the same good works—works of righteousness, obedience."

The second reference that used the "requirement in Eden" concept is found in Signs, September 5, 1892, and the theme was almost identical to what is found in the Steps to Christ reference just cited. The necessity for justification was prime, but the expression concluded with the thought that "justified by His grace" "good works will follow as the blossoms and fruit of faith."

These justificationist applications, however, did not dampen the ongoing expression of great possibilities for human achievement empowered by divine grace.

New Vehicles to Express Justification

What probably accounted for this revival and expansion of the perfectionist, transformationist use of this theme was a new concept that continued to find expression during the balance of Ellen White's ministry. It went like this:

Christ's merit and justifying work were seen as the keys to victory over sin in the life—not just a legal victory of pardon and justification, but the actual overcoming of sin in the life and character.

What Ellen White envisioned here is the Mary of Magdala response. The gracious deliverance of Jesus should always produce outpourings of lavish appreciation. How can my attitude to God be legal and behavioristic after I have felt His gracious and undeserved forgiveness?

What is going on in her thought at this critical juncture in her ministry needs careful analysis. Her vision of the intimate relationship of justification and sanctification has caused some well-meaning students of her writings to confuse the two. But Ellen White never did this, and her burden was always to make the proper distinctions. She did it, however, in ways that avoided extremes.

On the one hand, she shied away from a doctrine of salvation by the merit of imparted righteousness. On the other, she did not want to deny the powerful internal workings of God's Spirit, who makes Christ's righteousness real in our experience of obedience. In the next chapter we will carefully analyze some of her most doctrinally perplexing statements in order to see how she maintains gospel balance.

---

* Italics have been supplied in these quotations.

CHAPTER 13

Justification After Minneapolis—Maintaining Gospel Balance

S ome students of Ellen White, in their zeal to emphasize objective justification through the merits of Christ, have not wanted to recognize that Christ's "merits" are intimately involved in character development. Probably the most representative is Helmut Ott. "We should not take expressions such as 'union with Christ,' 'divinity and humanity combined,' and 'partaker of the divine nature' as references either to a pantheistic mixing of God and man or to a mystical blending of divine and human identities. The phrases are not suggesting a supernatural integration of human and divine natures, or some form of human deification" (68).

Ott here expresses a warning that has some validity in light of the pantheistic environment of late-nineteenth- and early-twentieth-century Seventh-day Adventist theological discussion. However, he takes it too far in restricting these expressions only to justification and imputation. "The believer 'becomes a partaker of the divine nature' when—and by reason of the fact that—he exercises 'faith in Christ, his atoning sacrifice.' Clearly, the righteousness of Christ is not a spiritual substance or a moral element that somehow gets infused into the believer" (*ibid.* 68).

For Ellen White there is never a meritorious infusion of righteousness, but righteousness certainly is active in the soul of the believer to beget righteous acts and character. It was clear to her that what was infused has no saving merit to justify the believer. The righteousness, how-ever, was certainly a "moral element that somehow" got "infused into the believer," according to Ellen White.

In principle, this ongoing expression was but a further clarification of the saved *from* sin, not *in* sin theme. Imputation was to be *distinguished* from impartation, but never *separated*. The people of God can experience real victory over sin only if they know that they are fully accepted in Christ's merits and righteousness.

Seemingly Inconsistent Statements

There were a few Ellen White statements that seem a bit doctrinally imprecise in their expression of the relationship between justification and sanctification.* They seem mainly to have been borne out of her deep desire to avoid the extremes of legalistic works of obedience and faith "alone" concepts that make the law of none effect.

The following is typical of such seeming imprecision: "Man cannot be saved without obedience" and "Christ should work in him to will and to do of His good pleasure" (RH, July 1, 1890). What she seemed to be suggesting was not works that have merit, but the clear understanding that with Christ's help, believers can develop characters fit for heaven.

This was all very closely related to the persistently stated theme of being saved *from* sin, not *in* it. This is clearly the intent of her statement in *Signs*, December 28, 1891: "Through obedience to all the command-ments of God, we are accepted in the Beloved." This seems quite legal-istic until the next paragraphs, where she states that "no one" with "an intelligent knowledge" of God's will "can be saved in disobedience."

Another interesting development that seemed to approve of theo-logical imprecision was her declaration that "many commit the error of trying to define minutely the fine points of distinction between justifica-tion and sanctification" (*1888 Materials* 897).

This seems to be a rather curious statement for Ellen White to make, because she had herself quite carefully defined the distinctions between justification and sanctification. But what she most likely had in mind were the dogmatic, strained definitions of extremist Seventh-day

Adventist minister E. R. Jones (not to be confused with his more well-known contemporary A. T. Jones).

She clearly rebuked Jones for trying to define "all the whys and wherefores as to what constitutes the new heart" or the "position" that "they can and must reach so as never to sin." She pointedly admonished him that he had "no such work to do" (1SM 177; we are not finished with the case of E. R. Jones and will meet up with him again in the next major section, which deals with perfection). This reference was written in May of 1890 and is the only statement that comes close to giving a hint as to what Ellen White was complaining about in the somewhat curious sounding manuscript 21, 1891.

Justification From 1893 Through 1902

The concepts of the right relationship between law and grace as well as faith and works were clearly reinforced but received no perceptible embellishment during this period from the perspective of the development of her doctrine of justification. The development of this concept of justification had reached its full maturity in the late 1888 through 1892 period.

Christ's Merits and Priestly Intercession

The quartet of ideas that grew out of her conception of the high priestly intercession of Christ unfolded along the following lines.

Christ's Merits Make Our Obedience Acceptable—The idea that the merits of Jesus make "the religious services" of believers acceptable to God continued to receive elaboration. But it was expressed not in new or original terms, but only in superbly comprehensive statements and concise clarity.

The consummate expression of the need for constant acceptance (and her expression of objective justification) came in the powerful statement of manuscript 50, 1900. To give the impact of its clarity and comprehensiveness, it is cited at length.

"Christ as high priest within the veil so immortalized Calvary that though He liveth unto God, He dies continually to sin, and thus if any man sin, he has an advocate with the Father. . . .

"Let no one take the limited, narrow position that any of the works of man can help in the least possible way to liquidate the debt of his transgression. This is a fatal deception. . . .

"This matter is so dimly comprehended that thousands upon thousands claiming to be sons of God are children of the wicked one, because they will depend on their own works. God always demanded good works, the law demands it, but because man placed himself in sin where his good works were valueless, Jesus' righteousness alone can avail. . . .

"No sin can be committed by man for which satisfaction has not been met on Calvary. Thus the cross, in earnest appeals, continually proffers to the sinner a thorough expiation. . . .

"As you come with humble heart, you find pardon, for Christ Jesus is represented as continually standing at the altar, momentarily offering up the sacrifice for the sins of the world. . . . A daily and yearly typical atonement is no longer to be made, but the atoning sacrifice through a mediator is essential because of the constant commission of sin. . . . Jesus presents the oblation offered for every offense and every shortcoming of the sinner" (1SM 343, 344).

It is clear that this powerful expression of objective justification referred primarily not to reprobates who had just come to Jesus for pardon, but to the ongoing needs of "true believers."

"The religious services, the prayers, the praise, the penitent confession of sin ascend from true believers as incense to the heavenly sanctuary, but passing through the corrupt channels of humanity, they are so defiled that unless purified by blood, they can never be of value with God. They ascend not in spotless purity, and unless the Intercessor, who is at God's right hand, presents and purifies all by His righteousness, it is not acceptable to God. All incense from earthly tabernacles must be moist with the cleansing drops of the blood of Christ. He holds before the Father the censer of His own merits, in which there is no taint of earthly corruption. He gathers into this censer the prayers, the praise, and the confessions of His people, and with these He puts His own spotless righteousness. Then, perfumed with the merits of Christ's propitiation, the incense comes up before God wholly and entirely acceptable. Then gracious answers are returned.

"Oh, that all may see that everything in obedience, in penitence, in praise and thanksgiving, must be placed upon the glowing fire of the righteousness of Christ. The fragrance of this righteousness ascends like a cloud around the mercy seat" (*ibid.* 344).

Christ's Merits Make Up for Our "Deficiencies"—The statements that spoke of Christ's merits acting as a buffer or safety net for human failure continued. "I rest in His love, notwithstanding my imperfections. God has accepted His perfection in my behalf." The very next paragraph continued with the admittance that "if we were perfect, we would not need a Saviour, a Redeemer to rescue us from the slavery of Satan" (letter 24, 1895, in 12 MR 35). They also showed no real development. Again it is clear that these expressions had come to full maturity in the 1889-1892 period.

Fending Off Satan's Taunting Accusations—The expression of dramatic dialogue, with penitent sinners responding to the taunts of Satan, the use of Zechariah 3, and the application of the proceedings of the investigative judgment to justification continued to be employed during this period, but with no discernible development.

Though the justificationist application of the investigative judgment was not very prominent after 1892 (even noticeable by its rare use), it did receive one very interesting use in 1893 in which the closely related themes of Christ's intercession with His merit and the work of judgment were tied together. "The work of God is to be carried on to completion by the cooperation of divine and human agencies. Those who are self-sufficient may be apparently active in the work of God; but if they are prayerless, their activity is of no avail. Could they look into the censer of the angel that stands at the golden altar before the rainbow-circled throne, they would see that the merit of Jesus must be mingled with our prayers and efforts, or they are as worthless as was the offering of Cain. Could we see all the activity of human instrumentality, as it appears before God, we would see that only the work accomplished by much prayer, which is sanctified by the merit of Christ, will stand the test of the judgment. When the grand review shall take place, then shall ye return and discern between him that serveth God and him that serveth Him not" (CS 263).

God's Willingness to Pardon—The expression of God's willingness to pardon sinners continued with numerous uses, but there was no discernible development compared with the previous period.

God's Infinite Requirements Necessitate Justification

The distinctive Ellen White concept that believers are required to meet the same standard as the unfallen Adam continued to find sparing but very important usage during this period. Furthermore, this thought seemed to be very closely associated with the increasing use of the idea that Christ's merits are the key to victory over actual sin and temptation in the believer's life. And all this was closely associated with the resurgence of emphasis on sanctification, character transformation, and perfection, which becomes patently evident in the last half of the 1890s and the first three years of the new century.

The idea that Christ's merits provide the basis of victory is quite understandable in the setting of her exposition of the profound balance between justification and sanctification. The thought here always seemed to be that believers just simply cannot begin to walk in the Christian life unless they know they are accepted in Christ through His merits.

The concept that believers must meet the same standard as the unfallen Adam was expressed in curious, seemingly contradictory ways.

How Are We "Justified by Perfect Obedience"?—The most perplexing statement of this concept came in 1901: "Only by perfect obedience to the requirements of God's holy law can man be justified. Let those whose natures have been perverted by sin ever keep their eyes fixed on Christ, the author and the finisher of their faith."

Five paragraphs later she said: "Those only who through faith in Christ obey all of God's commandments will reach the condition of sinlessness in which Adam lived before his transgression. They testify to their love of Christ by obeying all His precepts" (MS 122, 1901, in 8 MR 98, 99).

What makes this statement quite puzzling is its use of the word "justified," which seems to go contrary to her customary use of the term. She spoke of "perfect obedience" that justifies, an obedience that can be reached "through faith in Christ," an obedience that will "through faith" reproduce "the condition of sinlessness in which Adam lived before his transgression." *This is the most perplexing statement in all Ellen White's discussion of justification.*

If she had been required to stick to her own clear definition of "justified" and her overwhelmingly customary usage of it, then it is clear that what was manifested here was either a flat-out contradiction or possibly a lapse in precision.

Are We "Counted Precious" by "Imparted Righteousness"?—At least one other perplexing statement should be mentioned. She claimed that "it is only because of Christ's *imparted* righteousness that we are *counted* precious by the Lord" (RH, Aug. 24, 1897, italics supplied). Again it seems that her use of "imparted" was either a clear contradiction to customary meaning or a manifestation of imprecision. The latter seems to be the case in this sentence.

An Explanation of Perplexing Statements

What are we to make of these perplexing statements, especially the strongly worded phrase that "by perfect obedience to the requirements of God's holy law," man is justified?

In the setting of her overall usage, with an amazingly consistent expression of objective justification (throughout many years of ministry), this statement also seems to be a lapse in precision. It appears that the word "sanctified" would have fit much better. But could there be some deeper issue emerging in these statements?

It looks as if this emphasis on obedience and sanctified perfection was but a part of a larger movement in the unfolding of Ellen White's teaching on salvation. This larger movement seemed to reflect a growing fear that false definitions of faith were again looming as the larger threat.

Could it be that she sensed God's people making a subtle shift in attitude? Was faith being understood as mere mental assent, with no corresponding need to obey God's law? During this period the evidence certainly suggests that she felt the major enemy was not unwitting legalism but "believe, only believe" holiness perversions (real or perceived) that denied the importance of loving obedience.

It could be that what she was expressing in these seemingly imprecise and contradictory statements was her counterpart to the Epistle of James. "But wilt thou know, O vain man, that faith without works is dead? Was not Abraham our father justified by works, when he had offered Isaac his son upon the altar? . . . Ye see then how that by works a man is justified, and not by faith only" (James 2:20-24).

This was in contrast to the issues that brought on the crisis of Minneapolis and 1888. In that setting Ellen White gave Seventh-day Adventism her emphasis on the primary burden of Romans and Galatians. "Knowing that a man is not justified by the works of the law, but by the faith of Jesus Christ, . . . that we might be justified by the faith of Christ, and not by the works of the law: for by the works of the law shall no flesh be justified" (Gal. 2:16).

Whatever these statements meant in relationship to her exposition of justification, they were certainly forceful expressions of her ongoing delicate balance that sought to hold together merit and obedience, faith and works, law and gospel as the mutually complementary (not contradictory) essentials of salvation.

Summation of the Justification Development

While Ellen White's understanding of justification by faith was quite fully expressed by 1888 (especially between 1883 and 1888), the four years immediately following Minneapolis was the period of full maturity. It was a full maturity in the sense of greater clarity of expression and marked emphasis.

The late 1890s and the first three years of the new century witnessed a greater emphasis on the importance of obedience in relationship to justification. It was this expression that presented the most puzzling statements in Ellen White's literature on justification.

In the light of the dominance of emphasis on the importance of obedience throughout her ministry, it is probably appropriate that the developments of this post-Minneapolis era would climax with a return to an emphasis on perfection. With a grasp of her understanding of justification, we are now prepared to look at how her understanding of perfection unfolded.

---

*Some have even accused Ellen White of just plain inconstancy and contradiction. But I think the discussion in the next chapter will lay to rest this serious charge.

A Chronological Study

Section 4

PERFECTION

CHAPTER 14

Perfection Before 1888

We are now ready to tackle the most challenging part of Ellen White's teaching on salvation—perfection. Our purpose is to seek to understand how her view of perfection unfolded during the post-1888 era, the era of her greatest emphasis on justification. This will be the critical exhibit of her that we have been dealing with from the very beginning of her ministry.

The key question is How will the great surge of emphasis on justification affect the unfolding of her teaching on perfection for the balance of this post-1888 era? But before we examine the post-1888 era, it will prove helpful to trace her understanding of perfection as it unfolded throughout the years leading up to 1888.

Perfection, Sanctification, and Justification

For Ellen White, perfection was just about synonymous with sanctification. But we must always remember that perfection (no matter what it meant in any given passage) was the goal of sanctification.

In her thought justification and sanctification need to be *distinguished*, but not *separated*. The same goes for sanctification and perfection. Justification often defined perfection and always formed the foundation of the experience of sanctification. Sanctification often defined perfection, but at the same time perfection was always the goal of sanctification.

Sanctification and Perfection Before 1888

A number of different facets or characteristics go into Ellen

White's definition of perfection, and to get the full picture we need to understand each facet in its relationship to the whole. It is sort of like a great baseball team: there are star characters who really stand out, but the team is incomplete if a good supporting cast of characters on the bench is lacking. The whole team needs to be looked at, not just the outstanding players.

What follows is a review of all the essential "players" on Ellen White's "team" perfection.

The Goal and Attainment of Perfection

Probably the most striking features of Ellen White's presentation of the doctrine of perfection is the high goal to be attained and the many forthright, ringing declarations that its attainment is possible.

The Goal of Perfection—The following terms and expressions come from the entire pre-1888 era and express the goal of perfection in seemingly absolute terms.

"We can overcome. Yes; fully, entirely. Jesus died to make a way of escape for us, that we might overcome every evil temper, every sin, every temptation" (1T 144). "The Son of God was faultless. We must aim at this perfection and overcome as He overcame" (3T 336). Human beings can reach "a perfection of intelligence and a purity of character but little lower than the perfection and purity of angels" (4T 93). "All His righteous demands must be fully met" (RH, Aug. 23, 1881). "Every defect of character must be overcome, or it will overcome us, and become a controlling power for evil" (*ibid.*, June 3, 1884). "The law demands perfect, unswerving obedience" (TM 440). "Satan could find nothing in the Son of God that would enable him to gain the victory. . . . This is the condition in which those must be found who shall stand in the time of trouble" (GC 623).

In addition to these presumably absolute expressions, there were numerous strong presentations that believers, after the Fall, must meet the same standard as required of Adam before the Fall. She was explicit that God's requirement of "Adam in paradise before he fell" is just the same "at this moment" for all who live "in grace" (RH, July 15, 1890). She further enforced this by declaring that it is "not the work of the gospel to weaken the claims of God's holy law, but to bring men up where they can keep its precepts" (ibid., Oct. 5, 1886).

The various contexts of these statements make it clear that this is a requirement that is to be met in the believer's Spirit-empowered performance, not just through the accounting of Christ's perfect life of obedience to the penitent's account.

These are some of the strongest and most perplexing statements of perfection found in the writings of Ellen White. The key issue is whether her definition of perfection was qualified because of the sinfulness of human nature. We will deal more with this critical question a little later.

Another theme that expressed the high goal was her repeated employment of Matthew 5:48: "Be ye therefore perfect, even as your Father which is in heaven is perfect." Pointing to the importance of this theme, she clearly outlined the goal: "Holiness of heart and purity of life was the great subject of the teachings of Christ. In His Sermon on the Mount, after specifying what must be done in order to be blessed, and what must not be done, He says: 'Be ye therefore perfect, even as your Father which is in heaven is perfect.'

"Perfection, holiness, nothing short of this, would give them success in carrying out the principles He had given them" (2T 441).

Please note that "perfection and holiness" (apparently one and the same thing here) were not only the goal, but also the means of "success in carrying out the principles" of the Sermon on the Mount. A very similar expression was published in the Review of September 20, 1881: "'Be ye therefore perfect, [even] as your Father which is in heaven is perfect.' It should be our lifework to be constantly reaching forward to the perfection of Christian character, ever striving for conformity to the will of God. The efforts begun here will continue through eternity."

Thus it is clear that her comments on Matthew 5:48 were employed to express not only a high goal, but the dynamic means to reach this goal. Perfection was thus defined as both a goal and a relative experience that consists of pressing toward the goal. The concept she pictured here arises out of the whole experience of growth. The goal of growth is always maturity, but there is relative perfection at each stage of the dynamic unfolding.

The Attainment of Perfection—Not only was the demand and goal of perfection very high and seemingly absolute, but she also was very positive that this goal is attainable. Indeed, it must be attained this side of the close of probation and the glorification of the saints at the Second Coming.

There were numerous biblical witnesses whom Ellen White put forth as examples that such an attainment was possible this side of glorification, but her chief witness was Jesus Christ. His example became the key exhibit that she used to combat the challenge of her opponents that it is impossible for sinners to obey God's law perfectly. She saw this as one of Satan's great lies, and she clearly stated that Christ's sinless life is the answer to Satan's deceptive lie that perfect obedience is impossible.

Repeating an often-heard plea that "it's natural for me to be quick; it's my temperament," she responded by declaring that "all these 'natural' infirmities can be overcome by grace. . . . 'It's natural.' Satan loves to hear this." She then concluded with the strong affirmation that "Jesus says, 'My grace is sufficient for you'" (YI, November 1857). It is possible for penitent sinners to overcome temptations that appeal to both inherited and cultivated tendencies to evil, and there is no excuse for indulging in transgression.

Not only is there the example of Jesus in His humanity, but also there are those of Enoch, Daniel, Joseph, and Paul. All these Bible characters she regarded as positive, real-life demonstrations that it is possible for fallen humanity—through the grace and example of Jesus—to overcome fully.

The Distinguishing Qualities of Perfection

It is in this section that Ellen White's understanding begins to reveal its qualifying characteristics. In the previous section perfection was defined as seemingly absolute and attainable in this life by penitent sinners through Jesus' example and grace. But there were *distinguishing* and *qualifying* characteristics in her understanding of perfection!

Full Surrender—Perfection is an experience that arises out of *full surren-*

der and consecration to God's will and guidance in the life. No halfhearted commitment could attain the high goal of full and entire victory over sin.

Active Effort Required—The attainment of perfection is not a passive affair, but one that requires special effort on the part of the believer. There was no hint of "cruise control"* passiveness in Ellen White's sketch of Christian experience. Believers must move forward in faith at God's command and not idly lie back waiting for some special inspiration or shock treatment to move them to a life of vigorous character development.

The illustrative image which immediately comes to mind is the effort that the paralytic by the Pool of Bethesda needed to make in response to Jesus' command to get up and walk.

The Fruit of Dynamic Sanctification—Perfection is an experience that results from sanctification. Sanctification was understood to be *dynamic* and *progressive*—not static. Included in this expression was the closely related concept that sanctification is the "work of a lifetime." This, therefore, led to the very direct conclusion that sanctification is *not an instantaneous experience*.

No One to Claim Perfection—Closely related to the concept that sanctification is dynamic and progressive (and not instantaneous) was the clear warning that *no one is to claim perfection*. The reason for this warning arose primarily out of Ellen White's important insight into personal spirituality and the way sinful humans come to conviction of sin. The concept went essentially like this: the closer one comes to Christ, the clearer the vision of the divine perfection will be; consequently, there will be a greater realization of sinfulness, and the penitent one will have no desire to claim perfection.

For Ellen White, perfection, in at least some qualified sense, is attainable, but such an attainment for the spiritually perceptive Christian will always be a *consciously receding horizon* that can never be reached and claimed this side of glorification.

An Important Debate—Ellen White's interpreters disagree as to whether those who refuse to claim holiness or perfection are really sinlessly perfect or just being shy about their spiritual growth. Let us try to sharpen the focus on this issue with two questions: Is their refusal to claim perfection reflective of a truly realistic view that their perfection is relative, or are they truly sinlessly perfect and just being spiritually modest? Is the perfection they refuse to claim relatively sinless or absolutely sinless?

Dennis Priebe feels that "there can be a difference between being sinless and claiming to be sinless" (84). He bases this conclusion on Ellen White's statement which declared that "no one who claims holiness is really holy. Those who are registered as holy in the books of heaven are not aware of the fact, and are the last ones to boast of their own goodness" (ST, Feb. 26, 1885).

Helmut Ott seems to be more accurate in his appraisal of the numerous statements that Ellen White makes to the effect that holy saints have not, nor ever will, claim holiness or sinlessness. Referring to her statements that the saints will not claim "to be pure and holy" (GC 470) and noting their confession of a "sense of . . . weakness and imperfection" (PP 85), Ott comments: "Their admission of guilt and sinfulness did not result from a false sense of modesty or an inability to recognize their true spiritual standing. Instead, it rested on the fact that their unusually close relationship with God enabled them to acquire both the point of reference and the spiritual perception they needed to see themselves *as they really were*" (58, 59).

What they really were is perfect and holy in only a relative sense of the word, and this realization is the source of the reticence—not some sense of false modesty. Furthermore, they instinctively realize that to make a claim of perfection would even endanger the beauty of the relative reality! Sinful condition always plays a subtle trick on even religious persons: they are usually quite optimistic about their "own righteousness, which is of the law" (Phil. 3:9). Truly converted persons are much more sober about the reality of moral self-deception.

Perfection Accompanied by Strict Obedience—Sanctification and perfection involve a reverence for and strict *obedience to the law of God*. The focus here is the practical outworking of her firm conviction that believers are saved *from* sin, not *in* sin. Sinners are not saved by works, but neither are they saved without them (ST, July 13, 1888).

But she was careful in her emphasis on obedience to deny that this strict obedience was mere respectable morality or moralism. All true perfection must arise from an experience that senses a need for Christian conversion. "Some feel that they are almost right, because they do not commit outbreaking sins, and because they live moral lives. But all children, youth, middle-aged, and aged, have a work to do in taking the steps in conversion for which Jesus has given them an example in his life. . . .

"All who live have sins to wash away. They may have good intentions, and good purposes; they may have noble traits of character and live moral lives; notwithstanding, they need a Saviour" (YI, February 1874).

Symmetrical Obedience—A special feature of perfect obedience was that it should be *symmetrical*. This term refers to balance in carrying out God's will—not emphasizing one duty at the expense of another (3T 243ff.). She repeatedly sought to lead the faithful into an all-fronts battle against sin. "I know that those who bear the message of truth to them do not properly instruct them on *all points* essential to the perfection of a symmetrical character in Christ" (4T 314, italics supplied).

It is entirely possible that what she had in mind were the many people whom she met who made high claims to perfection and holiness, but whose personal lives were moral disasters.

The picture here is of tragicomic persons who do not understand the "weightier matters of the law" in their pathetic imbalance. They might be faithful in one area of devotion, but grossly negligent in others. Their health reform, for instance, "strains out gnats" while swallowing the "camels" of vegetarian gluttony. They are skilled in vegetable cookery but can easily become cannibalistic gourmets, feasting on the carcasses of their doctrinal opponents. They are experts at removing specks from the eyes of others while looking foolish with grotesque logs coming out of their own. Such lack of symmetry had no part in Ellen White's view of perfect obedience!

Perfect Believers Are Still Subject to Temptation—An experience of perfection does not mean that believers have reached the point of being free from temptations or totally above the possibility of sin. The perfect ones will be out of temptation's reach only after glorification (ST, June 9, 1881, and Mar. 23, 1888). Any claim to freedom from temptation this side of glorification is perfectionism, not a true perfectionist experience.

Feelings and Impressions Do Not Define Perfection—Sanctification and perfection were *not* to be *defined by feelings and impressions*. Feelings and impressions have their proper sphere, but are not the key determining factor of a genuine experience of perfection.

Impressions also included claims to be led of the Holy Spirit, especially if such pretensions conflicted with God's law or a plain scriptural principle (ST, Feb. 26, 1885). For Ellen White the business of religion was a very sober, no nonsense affair. Feelings and strong expressions of emotion received a rather skeptical review.

Here is another concept that clearly distinguishes Ellen White's view of perfection from the Wesleyan model. In her opinion the Wesleyan "witness of the Spirit" was too open to fanatical abuse. She urged believers to move forward in faith, trusting the clear promises of God's Word, not feelings and impressions.

The Perfect Ones Do Not Excuse or Cherish Sin—One of the most important qualities of a genuine experience of sanctification and perfection is that there will be *no cherishing, excusing, or indulging in sin*. This is closely related to her important distinction between willful, premeditated sinning and unwittingly being deceived or surprised into sin.

In the thought of Ellen White, no sin is excusable, but it is a vastly different spiritual psychology to sin willfully as opposed to being deceived or surprised into it.

It is very striking that many uses of the word "perfection" (and its variations) were often associated in the same context with an attitude that will not excuse or cherish sin of any kind—known or otherwise.

Such an association is strong evidence that for Ellen White perfection *negatively* meant the absence of (1) an attitude of excuse or cherishing sin and (2) the performance of willful and premeditated acts of sinning. *Positively* it meant doing the best one could do.

Maybe I can help you visualize the concept. I once lived in a rural setting in north central Georgia, where there were many logging trucks traveling the country roads. One morning I was running late to meet a radio appointment in town, and in my rush I ran into one of those trucks as it was coming around a blind corner. This accident was partly my mistake (as a result of my lack of punctuality), but I did not get up that morning longing to go out and purposefully ram the first logging truck I could find! My problem was a weakness, not an attitude. There is a world of difference.

Believer's Perfection Never Absolute—It should already be clear from the above discussion and from the presentations on justification in the previous chapter that perfection in the Christian experience is never absolute and can never be exactly the same as the experience and the perfection of Jesus. But the nonabsolute or relative nature of the believer's human perfection was further clarified in the following closely related ways.

1. Jesus is the only one who was absolutely perfect. In fact, Ellen White described those who claimed to be "equal with Him in perfection of character" as committing "blasphemy" (RH, Mar. 15, 1887). Compared with Christ, human perfection is always relative.

2. In addition to the comparison of human perfection with the absolutely perfect Jesus, the relative nature of the believer's perfection was expressed numerous times by Ellen White in simple, forthright ways to the effect that "you cannot equal the Pattern [Christ], but you can resemble it" (MS 32, 1887, 2 MR 126).

3. Aside from the more specific statements about the relative nature of perfection, there were numerous "His sphere, our sphere" statements. "As God Himself is perfect in His exalted sphere, so should His children be perfect in the humble sphere they occupy" (2SP 225). In relationship to defining the believer's perfection, it is not entirely clear what she was referring to in this expression.

She often used the "His sphere, our sphere" concept in commenting on Matthew 5:48. She seems to be referring to capabilities and powers (*1888 Materials* 146), which differ from person to person and certainly differ when the human is compared with the divine.

Though this "His sphere, our sphere" expression is a bit elusive, the gist of it seemed to be another way of saying that believers should do the best that they can with all the gifts, natural and supernatural, that are available to them in their sphere of existence. The bottom line, though, is that perfection is something different in God's sphere than it is in the human sphere.

Special Miscellaneous Characteristics—Ellen White occasionally lifted up for special treatment certain virtues, which mainly involve proper attitudes, the chief ones being humility and patience.

Another special feature was unity among believers. This accent on unity was probably because of a number of divisive and self-righteous critics of the Seventh-day Adventist Church who were claiming perfection, all the while creating strife in the church.

These three special characteristics need further comment.

1. Unity—Ellen White felt that the unity of believers would be an important hallmark of a true experience of sanctification and perfection. "Unity is the sure result of Christian perfection" (SL 85). False sanctification, on the other hand, seemed tailor-made to produce division, and she negatively referred to "those who accept this bogus sanctification [and] do not hesitate to draw away from the body and set themselves up as criteria." She went on to observe that "the very ones who claim sanctification have in their hearts insubordination, pride, envy, jealousy, and evil surmising of their brethren" (ST, Oct. 23, 1879).

2. Humility—"Those who experience the sanctification of the Bible will manifest a spirit of humility" (GC 470). This virtue was closely associated with the consciousness of not only creatureliness, but also sinfulness. Probably one of the reasons for her pointed rejection of the Wesleyan practice of claiming and testifying to the experience of perfection was that it was too easily subverted to manifestations of pretentious and false claims (*ibid.* 470-472; see 2T 638).

3. Patience—Without patience "we shall never reach a state of perfection" (HS 134).

The Means of Perfection

Though Ellen White spoke of making strenuous efforts in the life of sanctification, the effort was always conceived of as being empowered by God's grace. This grace was primarily ministered through the Word and the Spirit, working in intimate concert. This combined ministry would bring spiritual truth home to the individual heart in such a way that character transformation takes place.

Summation of the Pre-1888 Perfection Expressions

As Ellen White moved into the experience of Minneapolis and 1888, she had a complete and comprehensive doctrine of perfection. But the initial question of this chapter still calls for an answer. How did her understanding of perfection play out in the important years following 1888, which featured such a great emphasis on justification?

We will get to this question in chapter 16, but before we deal with it, there is one final issue that we need to address: How perfect is the perfection required of the saints who will make it through the time of trouble and will meet Jesus in peace at His second coming?

---

*I am indebted to Martin Weber for this wonderful metaphor.

CHAPTER 15

Perfection and Closing Events

Whenever a discussion of Ellen White and perfection arises, it is almost inevitable that the subject of the character perfection of God's people during the time of trouble will come up. As has already been pointed out in chapter 5, the perfection of the saints during this time is one of the most problematic areas in Ellen White's thought. In addition to the complex nature of her conceptions, the sinless perfection advocates consider her statement that God's people will have to "stand in the sight of a holy God without a mediator" (GC 425) to be one of the strongholds of their position. In other words, they understand Ellen White to be saying that God's people are so sinless that they no longer have sin in any shape or form and thus do not need Jesus' mediation.

Therefore we have devoted a whole chapter to a discussion of this rather challenging and important subject. But before we consider the character of the saints during the time of trouble, we should review some general considerations about the relationship of closing events to sanctification.

Fear and the Nearness of Christ's Coming

In the discussion about closing events in chapter 5 of this book, the basic relationship between a strong anticipation of Christ's coming and character development was outlined. From that discussion it is quite clear that Ellen White understood the "shortness of time" as a legitimate motivation for believers to perfect characters that would stand the scrutiny of the pre-Advent judgment, the rigors of the time of trouble, and the awesome presence of Jesus at His appearing. Ellen White, however, was not fond of fear as a primary motive in striving for character perfection.

Fear and Perfection—First of all, she declared that "the shortness of time is frequently urged as an incentive for seeking righteousness and making Christ our friend." But she went on to urge that "this should not be the *great* motive with us; for it savors of selfishness." She then asked: "Is it necessary that the terrors of the day of God should be held before us, that we may be compelled to right action through fear?" Her forthright answer was that "it ought not to be so" (ST, Mar. 17, 1887; italics supplied).

Thus despite the rather frightening descriptions of the awfulness of the close of probation, the time of trouble, and the day of Christ's personal appearing (GC 613-652), she could urge the "love, mercy, and compassion" of Jesus as one who will "walk with" believers and "fill" their "path with light" (ST, Mar. 17, 1887).

Complementing the theme of love (not fear) as the great motive were numerous statements urging that now—"today"—is the time of preparation for the trying times ahead. Typical of such expressions is the following.

"Live the life of faith day by day. Do not become anxious and distressed about the time of trouble, and thus have a time of trouble beforehand. Do not keep thinking, 'I am afraid I shall not stand in the great testing day.' You are to live for the present, for this day only. Tomorrow is not yours. Today you are to maintain the victory over self" (*ibid.*, Oct. 20, 1887).

The Investigative Judgment and the Time of Trouble

How do the closely related themes of the investigative judgment, the close of probation, and the character state of believers during the time of trouble contribute to an understanding of Ellen White's teaching on perfection?

Sanctification and the Investigative Judgment—Ellen White used the investigative judgment as a springboard to present the importance of both justification and sanctification. The theme is packed with motivational consequences and is another illustration of her gospel balance.

As a motivational factor for sanctification, she made numerous com
ments that speak of the close relationship between character purification
and the cleansing of the heavenly sanctuary. The following is typical:
"While the investigative judgment is going forward in heaven, while the
sins of penitent believers are being removed from the sanctuary, there is
to be a special work of purification, of putting away of sin, among God's
people upon earth. . . . When this work shall have been accomplished,
the followers of Christ will be ready for His appearing" (GC 425).

These comments sound almost as if there is some special dispensation of power associated with the period of the investigative judgment.
But Ellen White nowhere explicitly spoke of such a dispensation of special power that is to be uniquely available to the last generation. Such
power has always been available to believers.

Perfection and the Time of Trouble—Before we tackle this complex
and problematic issue, a brief outline of the way final events will unfold
is in order.

The close of probation signals the end of the pre-Advent, investigative judgment. This review of individual histories reveals to the universe
who will comprise the contrasting hosts of the redeemed and the lost.
The completion of the investigative judgment will then usher in the
close of probation, and it is at this time that the earth will be plunged
into the time of Jacob's trouble. This will be a most severe test of the en-
durance of the faithful.

What makes this whole sequence of events interesting is that from
God's point of view the personal salvation of the redeemed will no longer
be in question: they have been sealed with "the seal of the living God"—
an unseen mark that will certify their characters to be irreversibly set
(GC 613-615; 2T 191). But the sealed ones are not conscious of their
status before God. They will not know that they are sealed. They will be
involved in a terrible struggle of soul, seeking the assurance of sins forgiven and earnestly reviewing their life histories seeking to call up any
unconfessed sins. Ellen White is quite consistent in her concept that for
the faithful, perfection is always a consciously receding horizon—even
during the time of trouble (GC 616-622).

Ellen White's Most Perplexing Statement—But her most challenging and perplexing statement is that the sealed believers will have "to stand in the sight of a holy God without a mediator. Their robes must be spotless, their characters must be purified from sin by the blood of sprinkling" (GC 425).

What does it mean to live in the "sight of a holy God without a mediator"?

This question comes into sharp focus when we recall the powerful expression of objective justification involved in Ellen White's concept of Christ's ministry of mediation for believers. This intercession is not only needed to minister the benefits of redemption to the lost and alienated sinner, but was also deemed necessary to purify the earnest deeds of "true believers" from the "taint of earthly corruption." This was because such deeds had been done by "true believers" but who nevertheless still remained burdened with the "corrupt channels of humanity" (1SM 344).

So here are the "true believers" struggling through the most severe test of faith imaginable. Furthermore, in this brutal struggle they still possess mortal bodies that are oozing the "taint of earthly corruption" from their "corrupt channels." All that they do is "defiled" by "earthly corruption." Yet they have to struggle on "without a mediator"! What is to be made of all this?

Living Without a Mediator—First of all, let us be reminded that Ellen White was clear that the sealed believer's eternal destiny will not be at stake. All living humans will have conclusively and irrevocably chosen sides by the time probation closes. This is not because God makes some arbitrary decree, but because every person will have made a final choice to be loyal or lost. The close of probation simply confirms that the choices are now irreversible. So to live without a mediator means that the lost will no longer be able to switch sides.

While this point is relevant, it does not seem to speak to the main thrust of her perfectionistic comments in *The Great Controversy* about the time of trouble. It is true that there will be no switching sides, but the main thrust is not choice of salvation or damnation. The central issue is the perfection of the redeemed. Could it be that their charac-

ter will have become so perfect that they will have had their sinful natures, their corrupting channels, totally purged and eradicated as they
enter this crisis?

For Ellen White, the answer was negative. She never taught such a
perfectionism. She spoke of character perfection this side of glorification,
but not in terms of the final eradication of sinful nature. She clearly
stated that "we cannot say, 'I am sinless,' till this vile body is changed
and fashioned like unto His glorious body" (ST, Mar. 23, 1888, in 3SM
355). So the struggling, sealed believers retain their "vile bodies" with
their "sinful natures" (though they commit no acts of pre-meditated sin)
during the time of trouble.

What, then, did she mean when she spoke of a perfection that does
not need the mediation of Jesus? Does she mean that they will not need
Christ's grace or that Christ will no longer be sustaining them in their
severe trial? Will they have built up such a reservoir of grace *within* that
they will no longer have to look *without* to Christ?

If the answer is yes to these questions, then the entire thrust of Ellen
White's understanding of salvation would be severely distorted—even
stood on its head.

It would have been strange for one who had so consistently urged believers to look away from self and constantly to behold and trust in Jesus
as their advocate and mediator now to urge them to begin to look within
for some internal, subjective stockpile of strength.

This issue becomes especially acute when we realize that no one knows
the hour when probation closes. On this point Martin Weber has made
some cogent observations. "If we did not have access for forgiveness after
probation closes, and we did not know when that time arrived, how would
we know when to stop trusting in Jesus and start putting confidence in our
own character development? If so, would it not be dangerous to form the
habit of looking outside of ourselves to Jesus now, when we will shortly be
deprived of the privilege without knowing when?" (24, 25).

A Perfection That Needs No Mediation?—What is to be made of such
a perfection that does not need Christ's mediation?

I suggest a twofold answer.

First, *all restraints on evil are removed.* Among Ellen White's earliest comments about the time of trouble and the close of probation, she made it clear that the end of Christ's mediation signals the removal of all restraint on the evil passions of the lost (EW 279ff.; GC 613, 614).

Her description of the world during the time of trouble is nothing short of a dramatic horror thriller. The only restraint that will be placed on the satanically controlled hosts of the lost is that they will not be allowed to kill the "sealed ones" (GC 629-631). But beyond this the world is a living hell. To live without a mediator means to live by faith in a world that is spiritually and physically coming apart at the seams.

If believers have not exercised faith during their little, daily, probationary times of trouble, they will not have the experience to face this grand and horrible crisis. Yet even this still does not seem to get at what *The Great Controversy* (425) statement says about the perfection that will characterize the sealed believers.

Second, *we need a qualified understanding of perfection.* The explanation seems to arise out of Ellen White's understanding of perfection. God's sealed and faithful people are regarded as perfect in the sense that they are no longer cherishing sin or committing overt sins—sins that are deliberately or willfully performed. They will be imperfect in the sense that they still have sinful natures, so all that they do is less than the best. They still have unavoidable deficiencies, but they do not indulge in or commit premeditated acts of sin. Jesus is still making up for their "unavoidable deficiencies," "defects," "shortcomings," "mistakes,"[1] and "errors," but He is no longer mediating for the unsealed—the rebellious, willful, high-handed, sin-excusing sinners.

Let us carefully consider two lines of evidence for this interpretation: (1) repeatedly Ellen White suggested that the sins which are the major concern in character development are those that are willful, premeditated, cherished, indulged in, and excused; (2) it is striking how often the context of her time of trouble perfection descriptions spoke of or implied that perfection is an attitude that despises sin, avoids indulging in and cherishing it, and seeks the paths of obedience, doing the best that can possibly be done.

The reader should carefully observe the context of the statement about "the time when we are to confess and forsake our sins that they may go beforehand to judgment and be blotted out," the time when believers are to cleanse themselves "'from all filthiness of the flesh and spirit, perfecting holiness in the fear of God.'" The context of this statement also speaks in warning tones about indulging "one known sin" that "will cause weakness and darkness, and subject" believers "to fierce temptation" (HS 155).

In an obvious reference to the investigative judgment, she spoke of a "character that God can approve," "characters . . . printed upon the books of Heaven . . . [that] are fair and perfect." Then she urged that "it is our duty to render to God *the best service possible*" (ST, July 28, 1887; italics supplied).

During a sermon at Orebro, Sweden, in 1886, she spoke of "the Lord . . . weighing character in the sanctuary today, and those who are *careless and indifferent, rushing on in paths of iniquity*, will not stand the test" (*ibid.*, Dec. 29, 1887; italics supplied). She is clear that the type of character which will prove to be a failure is that which features carelessness and indifference to sin—"rushing on in paths of iniquity." This is a far cry from "unavoidable deficiencies" and "defects."

Note carefully the following reference, which seems to speak in the most absolute terms of the perfection of believers during the time of trouble. "Now, while our great High Priest is making the atonement for us, we should seek to become perfect in Christ. Not even by a thought could our Saviour be brought to yield to the power of temptation. . . . He had kept His Father's commandments, and there was no sin in Him that Satan could use to his advantage. This is the condition in which those must be found who shall stand in the time of trouble" (GC 623).

But right in the middle of this very absolute view of perfection she had this to say: "Satan finds in human hearts some point where he can gain a foothold; some sinful desire is cherished, by means of which his temptations assert their power" (*ibid.*).

Ellen White made it clear that the key issue in perfection and temptation is what to do with "sinful desire" that "is cherished." Doesn't it seem reasonable to conclude that if those who are cherishing sin will not make it, then the implication is that those not cherishing sin are the "perfect" believers who "stand in the sight of a holy God without a mediator" (ibid. 425)?

These sealed saints will have become so accustomed to trusting Jesus, loving the right, and cherishing obedience that they will no longer commit sins that need a mediator. Jesus will still be their mediator, in the sense of sustaining them in their weakness, but He will no longer intercede for those involved in rebellion and willful transgression.

Is not the issue the same now as it will be in the time of trouble? It seems clear that the issue is ceasing to indulge in or cherish sin. To put it plainly, the sealed will have ceased to do acts of willful sinning. For those who indulge sins and sinful attitudes, Jesus will no longer be able to mediate after probation closes; they are the high-handed sinners who stubbornly retain an unconverted heart.

A very similar thought is found in manuscript 26, 1888 (1888 Materials 161, 162). After speaking of what God and Jesus are doing in cleansing the sanctuary and the blotting out of sins, she asked: "Who expects to have a part in the first resurrection? You who have been cherishing sin and iniquity in the heart? You will fail in that day." Even though this speaks of those who will be resurrected, the same principle applies: no one who is cherishing known sin will be in God's kingdom.

That the believers are not absolutely, sinlessly perfect during the time of trouble (after probation ceases) was also hinted at in her comments in *The Great Controversy* on page 621. In an obvious reference to the condition of the sealed saints she said: "God's love for His children during the period of their severest trial is as strong and tender as in the days of their sunniest prosperity; but it is needful for them to be placed in the furnace of fire; *their earthliness* must be consumed, that the image of Christ may be *perfectly reflected*" (italics supplied).

It is clear that the sealed saints will not perfectly reflect (in the absolute sense) the image of Christ as they enter the time of trouble. Their eternal destiny will be settled, but their characters will still need to have "their earthliness . . . consumed"!

In light of Ellen White's overall understanding of the mental attitudes involved in both sin and righteousness, it seems consistent to understand the sealed saints as both perfect (not committing willful sins) and yet imperfect (not absolutely reflecting the perfect image of Jesus, because they will still need earthliness to be consumed).

God's Purpose for Time of Trouble

What is God's purpose in subjecting the sealed and judged saints to such a terrible ordeal?

First of all, the only explicit reason Ellen White gave for God's allowance of the time of trouble was consistent with her entire explanation for suffering (PP 68, 69, 78, 79; DA 19). God has permitted Satan to manifest the outworking of his principles since his fall, but during the time of trouble the sealed saints and the universe are given one last, full manifestation of evil (especially the death decree against the faithful saints) to demonstrate once and for all the horrible results of sin (Satan's principle) (PK 148).

Referring to the severe trials to be met in the time of Jacob's trouble, Ellen White specifically stated God's purpose: "It is designed to lead the people of God to renounce Satan and his temptations. . . . The last conflict will reveal Satan to them in his true character, that of a cruel tyrant, and it will do for them what nothing else could do, uproot him entirely from their affections" (RH, Aug. 12, 1884; OHC 321).

Two Conflicting Explanations

Aside from this one explicitly stated reason, her interpreters have come up with two quite different interpretations, which they feel are the point of her comments. These could be termed the perfectionistic and the justificationist interpretations.

The Perfectionistic Interpretation—Dennis Priebe's arguments are a good example of the perfectionistic interpretation. "I believe that the primary reason for a short delay before Christ's coming during which there is no Mediator is to dramatize before the watching universe the reality of God's complete power over sin in the lives of those whose wills are totally and forever united to His own. . . . The close of probation will play an important part in the final demonstration that God is making before His universe: that, indeed, it is possible for fallen man to obey God's law, which is righteous and good and holy" (86).

Is the main point of God here to demonstrate that the sealed ones can manifest perfect obedience to the universe in resisting the temptations of Satan? It appears that the major "temptation" which they "renounce" (OHC 321) will be the accusing assaults of the great adversary who seeks to lead them to distrust God's past pardon and mercy.

What is to be made of Priebe's interpretation?

First, his explanation is based on the theological premises of "final generation" theology, a school of thought in Seventh-day Adventist history which has contended that God absolutely needs a final generation of perfect saints to demonstrate that perfect obedience to the law of God is not just a possibility, but a reality.

Such theology has scant support in the writings of Ellen White, who held that Christ's life and death have once and for all settled the issue of whether humans can perfectly obey God's law.

Second, such a theology ignores a host of statements about the time of trouble which clearly declare that perfect obedience must be demonstrated *before* probation closes and the time of trouble begins.[2]

In other words, the essence of anything that Priebe could argue for has already taken place before probation closes. In fact, this is what the investigative judgment confirms: that God's living faithful are trusting and obedient and therefore can be sealed or certified as safe to save. That does not need to be proved during the time of trouble.

In Ellen White's thinking the larger issue of the possibility of obedience has been settled in Christ's incarnate experience; the issue of each individual person appropriating the merits of His life and death must be demonstrated before the close of probation and the conclusion of the investigative judgment—not during the time of trouble.

It would seem that what Priebe would contend for is that during the time of trouble the sealed saints must have further "earthliness . . . consumed." What God will seek to accomplish is not to test their loyalty in overt obedience, but to purify them further for His presence and that of the angels in the scenes of glory (GC 636).

The Justificationist Interpretation—Helmut Ott's position is a good example of the justificationist interpretation. It seems that he has clearly grasped the main purpose for God's allowance of the time of trouble. "Clearly, the trying experience [of] God's people" "reveals that they recognize their helplessness and unworthiness, that they have confessed their guilt and depend on God's forgiveness . . . , and that they do not yield to Satan's attempts to destroy their faith in God for deliverance" (117; see also 115).

Ott's suggestion is abundantly supported by Ellen White's treatment of the experience of Jacob as a type of the trials that God's sealed people will have during the time of trouble. The major theme of *The Great Controversy* treatment of this time is that they will cling by faith to God's mercy and His past pardon of their sins (616-622). The great trial for the sealed during the time of trouble is not temptation to commit open sins (*ibid.* 623), but to doubt God's acceptance through previous pardon for sins.

"They fear that every sin has not been repented of, and that through some fault in themselves they will fail to realize the fulfillment of the Saviour's promise: I 'will keep thee from the hour of temptation, which shall come upon all the world' (Rev. 3:10). If they could have the assurance of pardon they would not shrink from torture or death" (*ibid.* 619).

"They afflict their souls before God, pointing to their past repentance of their many sins, and pleading the Saviour's promise. . . . Their faith does not fail because their prayers are not immediately answered" (*ibid.* 619, 620).

"If the people of God had unconfessed sins to appear before them while tortured with fear and anguish, they would be overwhelmed; despair would cut off their faith, and they could not have confidence to plead with God for deliverance. But while they have a deep sense of their unworthiness, they have no concealed wrongs to reveal" (*ibid.* 620).

What the sealed ones will demonstrate is that they can cling by faith to God's mercy and pardon. The issue of their manifest obedience will have been settled before probation closes.

It appears that Priebe's perfectionistic bias has led him to miss the central point. He continues to discuss issues that were settled before probation closes, whereas God is seeking to demonstrate a faith in His mercy that will not be moved in the face of the most severe trial ever brought to bear on mortal flesh. In other words, the perfectionist appropriation of the time of trouble is quite at odds with its major purpose, which is to show forth God's great mercy and pardoning power in the lives of His loyal and sealed saints.

Summation

We now have a rather thorough picture of Ellen White's views on perfection as she approached the great watershed in the Adventist treatment of salvation. With these views in mind, we are now prepared to see how such concepts fared during the period of her greatest emphasis on justification by faith alone. Will her balancing act continue, or will her high doctrine of perfection be seriously qualified or compromised as she takes on the rampant legalism of a church in deep crisis?

---

[1] Ellen White in the *Review* of March 18, 1890, even implies that these "mistakes" of those who are "clothed with the righteousness of Christ" are "sins," but "sins" that are hated because they have caused the "sufferings" of God's Son.

[2] References to this full preparation before probation closes are in the following: *The Great Controversy*, pp. 425, 613, and 623: "Now, while our great High Priest is making the atonement for us, we should seek to become perfect in Christ;" *Early Writings*, p. 71; *Review and Herald*, Apr. 12, 1870, Aug. 12, 1884; *The Spirit of Prophecy*, vol. 3, pp. 40, 41; *Testimonies*, vol. 4, p. 429; vol. 5, pp. 220 and 466; *Signs*, Dec. 29, 1887; and *The Upward Look*, p. 192.

CHAPTER 16

Perfection After 1888

Probably the best way to trace Ellen White's views on perfection after 1888 is to use the same general categories that were used in chapter 14. We will now turn our attention to this vital subject as it unfolds in relationship to the great revival of emphasis on justification.

The Goal and Attainment of Perfection

During the entire post-1888 era Ellen White did not in the least blur her vision of the high goal of perfection that was attainable. Furthermore, she stated it in the most straightforward manner. She used all the same terms that she employed in the previous era, and there was no essential development that distinguished this era from the previous one.

What is most striking about this was that the high-demand goal continued to find strong expression in the immediate aftermath of the 1888 General Conference session. She did not slacken in her expression of the goal of God's high demand for character perfection.

The Distinguishing Qualities of Perfection

The development of her understanding of the distinguishing qualities of perfection was largely complete with the publication of *The Great Controversy* in 1888. This does not mean, however, that these qualities were ignored after 1888. They all received extended comment and discussion, but there was hardly any noticeable development of these concepts.

A Noteworthy Development—There was, however, a noteworthy development in the way the safety net or buffering concept was utilized. There was a noticeable decline in its use between 1896 and 1902.

It seems quite apparent that the emphasis on justification that began in earnest at Battle Creek in 1883 and reached floodtide in the aftermath of Minneapolis and 1888 was a notable motivation for these statements that recognized "unavoidable deficiencies." Of the 29 statements that speak to this issue from 1888 until late 1902, 16 came between 1889 and late 1892, 10 between 1893 and 1896, and none between 1896 and 1902. There were three published in 1902.

What should we make of this phenomenon? There seems little doubt that an emphasis on justification does tend to be more expressive of the inevitability of human failure. The powerful expressions of perfection that came between 1896 and 1900, on the other hand, seemed definitely to upgrade the possibility of human victory (by grace) over sin and downgrade the recognition of inevitable failure.

Yet we need to remind ourselves that just as perfection continued to be clearly taught right after 1888, so also justification was clearly taught during the last years of the 1890s and the early years of the twentieth century (witness the comprehensive manuscript 50, 1900 [1SM 340-344]).

The Natural or Spontaneous Vision of Perfection—One distinguishing quality that was only briefly mentioned before 1888 is an expansion of the whole concept that believers will not normally be conscious of their holiness. It is what could be called the natural, spontaneous, imperceptible nature of perfection.

The post-1888 expression of this quality was keynoted with the following statement. "*Imperceptibly* to ourselves, we are changed day by day from our own ways and will into the ways and will of Christ, into the loveliness of his character. Thus we grow up into Christ, and *unconsciously* reflect His image" (RH, Apr. 28, 1891; italics supplied).

The Desire of Ages in 1898 also presented this theme. "All true obedience comes from the heart. It was heart work with Christ. And if we consent, He will so identify Himself with our thoughts and aims, so blend our hearts and minds into conformity to His will, that when obeying Him we shall be but carrying out our own impulses" (668).

The Means of Perfection

The means of perfection received only one noticeable development after 1888—a strong emphasis on the transforming work of the Holy Spirit. Though this was not a new theme, it is clear that Minneapolis unleashed a veritable flood of statements to the effect that the Holy Spirit is the great bearer of power to transform lives into the image of Christ's perfection.

This theme was rarely mentioned before 1885, but I was able to locate 45 references to it after 1888. In fact, after 1888 it is mentioned at least once every year through 1902. What is interesting is that these statements were just as strong in the immediate aftermath of 1888 as they were in the late 1890s.

It should be recalled that it was during the late 1890s that Seventh-day Adventism was afflicted with the somewhat fanatical "Receive Ye the Holy Ghost" movement in North America. Ellen White had her own personal "Receive Ye the Holy Ghost" movement going in earnest for the balance of her ministry following 1888. Despite the extremes of the "Receive Ye the Holy Ghost" movement she moved ahead with a positive message of the power and work of the Holy Spirit to perfect believers.

Motivation for Perfection and the Investigative Judgment

By 1888 the basic theology of the investigative judgment was complete, with one notable exception. This was the troubling perfectionism of Seventh-day Adventist minister E. R. Jones.

In 1890 Jones was teaching a version of perfection which claimed that before the close of probation "God's people can and must develop a personal righteousness that is as radical and complete—and . . . as meritorious—as that of Christ" (Ott 131, cf. 137, 138). Whatever it was, Ellen White was not very taken with it. In fact, she called him an extremist. "Some ministers like Edwin Jones can never take a position and hold it sensibly. He will regard matters in an intense light. He will gather up little points of seeming difference and act as though he would stake his soul upon their verity and strength . . . He confuses minds, he buries the simplest and most essential truths by his strong expressions, his extravagant imaginations so that his labors on this coast [Pacific] are really a failure" (letter 46, 1890, in *1888 Materials* 646, 647).

Her counsel to Jones was direct. "It is not essential for you to know and tell others all the whys and wherefores as to what constitutes the new heart, or as to the position they can and must reach so as never to sin. You have no such work to do" (letter 15a, 1890, in 1SM 177).

"You will take passages in the Testimonies that speak of the close of probation, of the shaking among God's people, and you will talk of a coming out from this people of a purer, holier people that will arise. Now all this pleases the enemy. . . .

"Should many accept the views you advance, and talk and act upon them, we would see one of the greatest fanatical excitements that has ever been witnessed among Seventh-day Adventists. This is what Satan wants" (*ibid.* 179).

The judgment and the close of probation are proper motivators for character perfection, but extremists who wanted to go beyond character perfection into nature perfection were sharply rebuked. It is quite apparent that Ellen White did not want the perfectionistic implications of the judgment and the close of probation developed any further than she had taken them in *The Great Controversy*.

The Relationship of Justification and Sanctification

One of the most notable qualities of Ellen White's thought on the motivation for character perfection during the post-1888 era was the great emphasis on merit and justification as the root or foundation for victory over sin.

This theme was stated sparingly before 1888. Probably the clearest pre-1888 statement was made at the important (and often overlooked) 1883 Battle Creek General Conference session. "When we trust God fully, when we rely upon the merits of Jesus as a sin-pardoning Saviour, we shall receive all the help that we can desire" (RH, Apr. 15, 1884).

This 1883 expression was later strengthened with her comments about Wesley's conversion. "He continued his strict and self denying life, not now as the *ground*, but the *result* of faith; not the *root*, but the *fruit* of holiness" (GC 256).

It was after 1888, however, that this theme was repeatedly mentioned in both justificationist and sanctificationist settings. It was not so much that the theme was any more clearly expressed, but that it was expressed so often. The initial statement of this concept during the 1889-1902 era was quite typical of the host of comments that followed.[1] Referring to the testimonies of the delegates at the 1889 Battle Creek General Conference session, she made this comment: "All related their experience the past year as being of a more spiritual character than they have had before since embracing the truth. The light of justification through faith, and that the righteousness of Christ must become our righteousness, else we cannot possibly keep the law of God, is the testimony of all who speak, and the fruit is peace, courage, joy, and harmony" (MS 22, 1889, in *1888 Materials* 461).

In the opinion of Ellen White the spiritual impact of 1888 had been most positive. And this theme continued to receive great and constant emphasis from her pen and voice for the balance of her ministry. Such constant emphasis of the root/fruit relationship of justification and sanctification presents abundant evidence of the centrality of the justification/sanctification balance in her thought. This delicate balancing was evident after 1888—during the periods of emphasis on both justification (1889-1892) and sanctification (c. 1895-1902).

Summation of the Perfection Development

The development of all Ellen White's various understandings of perfection was essentially complete by 1888. Only a few features of her doctrine of perfection received further expansion. This did not mean, however, that the doctrine was downgraded. In fact, the opposite was true.

Two other developments gave evidence of this tilt toward perfection in her attempts at balance.

1. As discussed earlier, the years 1901 and 1902 witnessed a strong revival of the spirit of the New Testament Epistle of James. This revival found its most forceful pronouncement in the perplexing statement pub-

lished in the *Signs* of July 23, 1902: "But by perfect obedience to the requirements of the law, man is justified. Only through faith in Christ is such obedience possible."

It is not entirely clear what provoked this rather uncharacteristic use of the term *justified*, but it certainly did evidence the great emphasis on obedience and character development in her teachings on salvation.

2. The last exhibit was the way she often described sanctification and perfection as the definition or major purpose of religion. This theme was clearly stated before 1888. "Holiness of heart and purity of life was the great subject of the teachings of Christ. . . .

"Perfection, holiness, nothing short of this, would give them success in carrying out the principles He had given them" (2T 445).[2]

But this was repeatedly mentioned in the post-1888 era, with most of the emphasis coming after 1897. The expression of this theme was climaxed with two strong statements in 1902: "Our sanctification is God's object in all His dealing with us. He has chosen us from eternity that we may be holy" (letter 153, 1902, in 3SM 202). "The history of Christ's human life in our world is the record of His purpose toward us for the manifestation of His divine perfection" (RH, Oct. 14, 1902). Such expressions certainly summarize the thrust of Ellen White's understanding of perfection.

The delicate balance between justification and sanctification was a constant given throughout her entire ministry, but her teaching, with its ongoing emphasis on character transformation, is most aptly summed up as "the persistent path to perfection." Even during the period of her greatest accent on objective justification, such emphasis was always the stepping-stone to the ultimate prize—the reflection of the perfect character of Jesus in Christian experience.

---

[1] Fifty-seven separate statements of this theme were located in the 1889-1902 era, with numerous statements appearing each year.

[2] This statement was republished verbatim in the *Review*, Sept. 7, 1886.

Section 5

An Interpretation

CHAPTER 17

What Does It All Mean?

With all the discussion and debate about Ellen White's views on justification and perfection, I feel the reader is entitled to know what this study has contributed to my thinking on these vital issues. I will not review the development of her teachings in this final chapter. That can be traced in the periodic summations scattered throughout the previous chapters. But for the sake of clarity and some further expansion, I suggest the following interpretation.

Justification

It is clear that Ellen White's understanding of justification by faith had almost every legal or objectively forensic element that the sixteenth-century Reformers Martin Luther and John Calvin argued for. Although her understanding of salvation sounds more like Wesley's emphasis than that of the earlier Reformers, she did go beyond Wesley in declaring that Christ's life and death must be accounted to believers all the way, not just at the beginning of Christian experience. In other words, justification is always concurrent with sanctification.

John Wesley and Ellen White—Wesley was wary of the view that both the life and death of Christ are legally accounted to the records of believers, feeling that such a view would deny the necessity of sanctification and perfection. But Ellen White had no such reservations. Her 1883 and post-1888 explanations of justification by faith were powerfully clear statements of justification defined as God's act in declaring penitents to be free from condemnation.

Ellen White's presentation of salvation was a feast that consisted of all the redemptive delights that both the Lutheran and Wesleyan traditions have passionately hungered for, with very little dislike for what they both tended to neglect or downgrade.

Believers Justified Every Moment—At the risk of being repetitious, let us get it clear in our minds: the moment a sinner repents and confesses, that moment he or she stands forth fully accepted in the Beloved by the merits of Christ's life and death ministered through His constant and objective heavenly intercession. By faith, *every moment* believers are reckoned perfect in Christ Jesus: not on the basis of their performance, but through Christ's gracious and meritorious accounting.

It is usually this theme that the strong advocates of perfection need to pay attention to with greater care. Do we really believe that Jesus accepts us fully and completely through His merits alone?

Faith and Obedience—But such an experience of justification is retained only on the basis of faithful loyalty to Christ, which is expressed in constant obedience and repentance. It is this side of the balance that the justification advocates usually need to concentrate on with more care. Such obedience, however, is the best that believers can do by God's grace, and Ellen White never understood such obedience as generating saving merit.

It seems that the best way to sum up the balance in Ellen White's teaching on faith, merit, and obedience goes like this: believers are justified *evidentially* by works of perfect obedience. But they can be justified *meritoriously* only by faith in the merits of Christ, which He accounts to us by His constant intercession. Sinners are saved in *experience* by faith, *in merit* by the grace of Christ accounted to us, and obedience is the essential *evidence* of faith's acceptance of Christ's precious merits.

Perfection

The word "perfection" is often thought of as only applying to absolute, antiseptic sinlessness—nothing less, nothing more. Such a view is static and usually deals only with specific actions, habits, and behavior. But Ellen White's thought is more realistic and complex than such simplistic notions.

Her views on perfection reveal a wonderfully balanced outline that features six levels of experience. These levels logically follow one after the other. To remove them from their place in the sequence or to deny any one of them is to distort the balance of the whole picture.

This wonderfully panoramic vision goes like this:

1. *Reckoned Perfect*—The moment we repent and trust the saving merits of Christ, that moment we are *reckoned* as completely perfect in Him. His perfection is ours by faith, despite past sins and present, unwitting failures.

2. *Dynamic Growth Seen as Relative Perfection*—If we are moving forward by faith, growing in grace, and developing characters patterned after the likeness of Christ, we are *relatively* perfect at every stage of growth. We are inevitably deficient and immature, but such growing (though immature) believers are nonetheless perfect. A plant is perfect at each stage of its development, despite its lack of full maturity. In sum, perfection is *dynamic growth* in attitude and actions.

3. *Loving Obedience and No Willful Sinning*—It is possible for us to reach a level of maturity that will finally feature a constant and *spontaneous manifestation of loving obedience* to all the will of God and a noticeable *lack of manifest sinning*. The key features of such a level of maturity are:

a. We will not be conscious of any absolute perfection. The closer we come to Christ and His perfection, the greater will be our realization of our own defects.

b. Perfection is all possible obedience to God's will in probationary time. This obedience is produced by the right use of the will in cooperation with the empowerment of divine grace.

c. There will be neither cherishing of sin, nor rebellious attitudes of presuming on God's grace by willful disobedience. John Fowler suggests that such a person is "sinful by nature" but "is not sinning in deliberate violation of God's law" (Fowler 148). In a word, there will be no premeditated sinning.

d. Perfection has been, and always will be, a consciously receding horizon and never claimable in this mortal sphere. Here she was in direct conflict with the Wesleyan expectation that sinners could claim conscious and instantaneous victory over known sin. And the reason for this is that Wesley's ultimate definition of perfection was that it was victory over known sin. For Ellen White, perfection did involve victory over known sin, but it was a deeper, more all-encompassing vision.

R. N. Flew raises a warning flag about a common pitfall in the experience of perfection. He suggests that if known transgression is the only object of sanctification, then perfection will depend on our "own insight into" our motives, previous moral development, and our "knowledge" of ourselves. All this is very shaky ground for claiming perfection, and Flew's comments are powerfully insightful.

"Many otherwise good people are unconscious of their own selfishness. The quarrelsome man genuinely thinks that everyone is unreasonable but himself. The revengeful man believes that he is animated only by a proper self-respect. . . .

"These considerations which hold good even of the commoner vices, the more flagrant sins, are true of the subtler and more deadly sins of the spirit. Pride in all its forms, vanity, egotism, spiritual complacency, a self-centered religion, the pharisaism which is goodness, and yet is false goodness—all these forms of moral evil are most likely to appear in those whose lives are disciplined and virtuous" (Flew 333).

Flew's criticism of Wesley could never be directed at Ellen White. Her stress was always on the dynamic aspects, and sanctification was always called "the work of a lifetime."

Furthermore, Ellen White's understanding of the demands of God's law and her view of the pervasiveness of sin as a deranging power in the human soul was more concrete and radical than Wesley's.

4. *Perfection in the Time of Trouble*—Her descriptions of the experience of the sealed and loyal saints during the time of trouble following the close of human probation seem to represent an understanding of perfection that is very closely related to point 3 above. Yet her descriptions speak of a total lack of blatant sinning during this period. It is this total lack of open, identifiable sinning that distinguishes the perfection of the loyal during the time of trouble from their experience before probation closes.

What is certain is that there will be no manifestations of premeditated sinning during the time of trouble, and God's people can recall no sins that have not been repented of and forsaken. While they are not aware of any conscious sins, they do have further "earthliness" to be removed during this terrible ordeal.

While it is not entirely clear if they will or will not be committing "errors," "mistakes," and manifesting "unavoidable deficiencies" during this time, W. Richard Lesher has probably summed it up best when he declared that for Ellen White individuals are "sinner[s]" though they may not "always" be "sinning" as "a practicing sinner" (Lesher 246). Such is certainly true of the saints during the time of trouble.

5. *Sinless at Glorification*—Perfection in the fullest sense of the word "sinless" comes for the first time at the appearing of Jesus, when we will receive immortality and will no longer be subject to the passions of the sinful nature and Satan's deceptive temptations of Satan.

6. *Constant Growth Throughout Eternity*—Perfection will continue to manifest itself as constant growth into the likeness of Christ's character through all eternity.

Perfectionist or Perfectionism?

Ellen White was certainly a perfectionist, but she was not advocating perfectionism.

I am using the expression *perfectionist* in the sense that sinners can gain victory over sinful attitudes and actions, but they retain their corrupt natures, which are subject to temptation until glorification. They experience victory over hereditary and cultivated tendencies to sin, but the propensities and tendencies are never wholly removed till the Second Coming.

Perfectionism, on the other hand, involves believers coming to the place where, before glorification, they would no longer feel the effects of temptation. In other words, they would have not only transformed characters, but also their sinful natures would be eradicated. Clearly this was not Ellen White's position.

A Gracious Optimism

Ellen White was most optimistic about what could be accomplished when the human will is combined with divine power. Great heights of character development will result. And can we not call this good news?

I am personally thankful that I do not have to be burdened with any hereditary or cultivated defect. Certainly there is victory not only from the guilt of but also the power of sin!

For Ellen White, salvation was the persisting path to personal character perfection. All her theological resources were brought to bear on this central theme, and no aspect of her instruction was lacking in its doctrinal and practical applications.

BIBLIOGRAPHY

I. Ellen White Material

The Acts of the Apostles. Mountain View, Calif.: Pacific Press Pub. Assn., 1911.

The Adventist Home. Nashville: Southern Pub. Assn., 1952.

The Bible Echo (periodical): Not yet released in facsimile edition.

Child Guidance. Nashville: Southern Pub. Assn., 1954.

Christian Experience and Teachings of Ellen G. White. Mountain View, Calif.: Pacific Press Pub. Assn., 1922.

Christian Service. Washington, D.C.: Review and Herald Pub. Assn., 1940.

Christ's Object Lessons. Washington, D.C.: Review and Herald Pub. Assn., 1941.

Colporteur Ministry. Mountain View, Calif.: Pacific Press Pub. Assn., 1953.

Counsels on Diet and Foods. Mountain View, Calif.: Pacific Press Pub. Assn., 1938.

Counsels on Health. Mountain View, Calif.: Pacific Press Pub. Assn., 1923.

Counsels to Parents, Teachers, and Students. Mountain View, Calif.: Pacific Press Pub. Assn., 1943.

Counsels to Writers and Editors. Nashville: Southern Pub. Assn., 1946.

The Desire of Ages. Mountain View, Calif.: Pacific Press Pub. Assn., 1898.

Early Writings. Washington, D.C.: Review and Herald Pub. Assn., 1945.

Education. Mountain View, Calif.: Pacific Press Pub. Assn., 1952.

The Ellen G. White 1888 Materials, (facsimile reproductions). Washington, D.C.: Ellen G. White Estate, 1987. 4 vols.

Evangelism. Washington, D.C.: Review and Herald Pub. Assn., 1946.

Faith and Works. Nashville: Southern Pub. Assn., 1979.

Fundamentals of Christian Education. Nashville: Southern Pub. Assn., 1923.

General Conference Bulletin, 1891, 1893, 1897, 1899, 1900, 1901, 1903, 1909, 1912. Silver Spring, Md.: Department of Archives and Statistics, General Conference of Seventh-day Adventists.

Gospel Workers. Washington, D.C.: Review and Herald Pub. Assn., 1948.

The Great Controversy. Mountain View, Calif.: Pacific Press Pub. Assn., 1911.

Health, or How to Live. Battle Creek, Mich.: Steam Press of the Seventh-day Adventist Pub. Assn., 1865.

Historical Sketches of the Foreign Missions of the Seventh-day Adventists. Basel, Switzerland: Imprimerie Polyglotte, 1886.

In Heavenly Places. Washington, D.C.: Review and Herald Pub. Assn., 1967.

Life Sketches. Mountain View, Calif.: Pacific Press Pub. Assn., 1943.

Manuscript Releases. Silver Spring, Md.: Ellen G. White Estate, 1981-1993.

Medical Ministry. Mountain View, Calif.: Pacific Press Pub. Assn., 1963.

Messages to Young People. Nashville: Southern Pub. Assn., 1930.

Mind, Character, and Personality. Nashville: Southern Pub. Assn., 1977. 2 vols.

The Ministry of Healing. Mountain View, Calif.: Pacific Press Pub. Assn., 1909.

Our High Calling. Washington, D.C.: Review and Herald Pub. Assn., 1961.

Patriarchs and Prophets. Mountain View, Calif.: Pacific Press Pub. Assn., 1890.

Paulson Collection. Payson, Ariz.: Leaves-of-Autumn, n.d.

Prophets and Kings. Mountain View, Calif.: Pacific Press Pub. Assn., 1916.

Review and Herald Articles (facsimile reprint). Washington, D.C.: Review and Herald Pub. Assn., 1962. 6 vols.

The Sanctified Life. Washington, D.C.: Review and Herald Pub. Assn., 1937.

Selected Messages. Washington, D.C.: Review and Herald Pub. Assn., 1958; 1980. 3 books.

Sermons and Talks. Silver Spring, MD.: Ellen G. White Estate, 1990.

The Seventh-day Adventist Bible Commentary. Ellen G. White Comments. Washington, D.C.: Review and Herald Pub. Assn., 1952-1957. 7 vols. (including vol. 7-A). (Volume 7-A contains in one convenient setting all the Ellen White Comments that come at the end of each volume of the seven volumes of commentary. It also contains the Ellen White collection of primary references from the three appendices of *Seventh-day Adventists Answer Questions on Doctrine*.)

Seventh-day Adventists Answer Questions on Doctrine. Washington, D.C.: Review and Herald Pub. Assn., 1957. (Appendices A, B, and C contain an important collection of primary references from Ellen White's published and unpublished writings.)

Signs of the Times Articles (facsimile reproductions). Mountain View, Calif.: Pacific Press Pub. Assn., 1974. 4 vols.

A Sketch of the Christian Experience and Views of Ellen G. White. Saratoga Springs, New York. James White, 1851. (Now, with revisions, it is in *Early Writings*).

Sons and Daughters of God. Washington, D.C.: Review and Herald Pub. Assn., 1955.

The Spirit of Prophecy (facsimile reproduction). Washington, D.C.: Review and Herald Pub. Assn., 1969. 4 vols.

Spiritual Gifts (facsimile reprint). Washington, D.C.: Review and Herald Pub. Assn., 1945. 4 vols.

Steps to Christ. Mountain View, Calif.: Pacific Press Pub. Assn., 1956.

A Supplement to the Experience and Views. Rochester, New York: James White, 1854. (Now in *Early Writings*.)

Testimonies for the Church. Mountain View, Calif.: Pacific Press Pub. Assn., 1948. 9 vols.

Testimonies to Ministers and Gospel Workers. Mountain View, Calif.: Pacific Press Pub. Assn., 1923.

That I May Know Him. Washington, D.C.: Review and Herald Pub. Assn., 1964.

Thoughts From the Mount of Blessing. Washington, D.C.: Review and Herald Pub. Assn., 1955.

The Upward Look. Washington, D.C.: Review and Herald Pub. Assn., 1982.

Welfare Ministry. Washington, D.C.: Review and Herald Pub. Assn., 1952.

Youth's Instructor Articles (facsimile reproductions). Washington, D.C.: Review and Herald Pub. Assn., 1986.

Note: The Ellen White writings feature numerous unpublished manuscripts and letters. Many of these have been printed in different publications, as have many of the periodical articles. Any manuscript, periodical article, or letter that does not have a published reference is on file at the Ellen G. White Estate in Silver Spring, Maryland.

II. Other Sources

Daniells, A. G. *Christ Our Righteousness*. Washington, D.C.: Review and Herald Pub. Assn., 1926.

Delafield, D. A. *Ellen White in Europe*. Washington, D.C.: Review and Herald Pub. Assn., 1975.

Fernandez, Gil G. "Ellen G. White: The Doctrine of the Person of Christ." Ph.D. dissertation, Drew University, 1978.

Flew, R. Newton. *The Idea of Perfection*. London: Oxford University Press, 1934.

Fowler, John. "The Concept of Character Development in the Writings of Ellen G. White." Ed.D. dissertation, Andrews University, 1977.

Froom, L. E. *Movement of Destiny*. Washington, D.C.: Review and Herald Pub. Assn., 1971, 1978.

Graham, Roy E. *Ellen G. White: Co-Founder of the Seventh-day Adventist Church*. New York: Peter Lang, 1985.

Guy, Fritz. "The Ultimate Triumph of Love: An Adventist Understanding of Atonement." Unpublished paper, late 1970s.

Haloviak, Bert. "Bookshelf: Review of George R. Knight's From 1888 to Apostasy: The Case of A. T. Jones." *Focus*, Winter 1988/1989, p. 24.

———. "From Righteousness to Holy Flesh: Disunity and the Perversion of the 1888 Message." Unpublished manuscript, Office of Archives and Statistics, General Conference of Seventh-day Adventists, Washington, D.C., April 1983.

———"From Righteousness to Holy Flesh: Judgment at Minneapolis." Unpublished book manuscript, privately held by the author and with a copy given to this researcher, Washington, D.C., 1988.

———. "Pioneers, Pantheists, and Progressives: A. F. Ballenger and Divergent Paths to the Sanctuary." Unpublished manuscript prepared for the Glacier View Conference, August 1980, by Office of Archives and Statistics, General Conference of Seventh-day Adventists, Washington, D.C., June 1980.

Knight, George. *From 1888 to Apostasy: The Case of A. T. Jones*. Hagerstown, Md.: Review and Herald Pub. Assn., 1987.

LaRondelle, Hans K. *Perfection and Perfectionism*. Berrien Springs, Mich.: Andrews University Press, 1971.

Lesher, W. Richard. "Ellen G. White's Concept of Sanctification." Ph.D. dissertation, New York University, 1970.

Maxwell, A. Graham. *Servants or Friends*. Redlands, Calif.: Pineknoll Pubs., 1992.

Moore, A. Leroy. *Theology in Crisis*. Corpus Christi, Tex.: Life Seminars, 1980.

Neall, Ralph E. "The Nearness and the Delay of the Parousia in the Writings of Ellen G. White." Ph.D. dissertation, Andrews University, 1982.

Olson, Robert. "Outline Studies on Christian Perfection and Original Sin." *Ministry Supplement*, October 1970.

Ott, Helmut. *Perfect in Christ*. Hagerstown, Md.: Review and Herald Pub. Assn., 1987.

Poehler, Rolf J. "Sinless Saints or Sinless Sinners? An Analysis and Critical Comparison of the Doctrine of Christian Perfection as taught by John Wesley and Ellen G. White." Research paper, Andrews University, April 1978.

Priebe, Dennis E. *Face to Face With the Real Gospel*. Boise, Idaho: Pacific Press Pub. Assn., 1985.

Schwarz, Richard W. *Light Bearers to the Remnant*. Mountain View, Calif.: Pacific Press Pub. Assn., 1979.

Seventh-day Adventists Answer Questions on Doctrine. Washington, D.C.: Review and Herald Pub. Assn., 1957.

Wallenkampf, Arnold V., and W. Richard Lesher, eds. *The Sanctuary and the Atonement*. Washington, D.C.: Review and Herald Pub. Assn., 1981.

Weber, Martin. *Vindication*. Anaheim, Calif.: Privately published, 1981.

Webster, Eric C. *Crosscurrents in Adventist Christology*. New York: Peter Lang, 1984.

Wesley, John. *The Works of John Wesley* (Jackson Edition). Peabody, Mass.: Hendrickson Pub., Inc., 1984. 14 vols.

———. *The Works of John Wesley*. Ed. Albert Outler (Bicentennial Edition). Nashville: Abingdon, 1984-1987. Vols. 1-4.

White, Arthur L. *Ellen G. White*. Washington, D.C.: Review and Herald Pub. Assn., 1981-1986. 6 vols.

Wieland, R. J. *An Introduction to the 1888 Message Itself*. Baker, Ore.: Adventist Forum Assn., 1976.

———. *The 1888 Message: An Introduction*. Nashville: Southern Pub. Assn., 1980.

Wieland, R. J., and Donald K. Short. *1888 Re-Examined* (revised and updated). Leominster, Mass.: Eusey Press, 1987 (released under the auspices of "The 1888 Message Study Committee").